A GOSPEL ENCOUNTER

100 DAILY DEVOTIONS

KYLENE CROSSEN

Let me tell you about my Jesus...

Kylene Crossen
Psalm 51:10
♡

Photography by
KYLENE CROSSEN

ISBN: 978-1-7374707-1-7
eBook ISBN: 978-1-7374707-0-0

Published by Kylene Crossen
xrossenministries888@gmail.com

Cover layout design by sam_4321 at Fiverr
Cover photo by Kylene Crossen

The forms LORD and GOD used in Bible quotations represent the Hebrew name for God Yahweh (Jehovah). Lord and God represent the name Adonai. I have used the form found in the Bible that the quote was taken from.

100 DAILY DEVOTIONS
Journey along and discover the hidden things of God

This book is dedicated to God my Father, Son and Holy Spirit.

I thank you Abba Father for sending me your one and only Son Christ Jesus. He lovingly became my Savior and my redeemer. The Holy Spirit became my  *helper and comforter. He has continuously guided, guarded, directed and protected me. I am who you say I am. When I went lost and astray, you journeyed to the ends of the earth to find me. It is by your grace and mercy that I can stand upright today. When I became an orphan, you prepared a place for me. You saved me from myself and showed me how a Father truly loves a daughter. You placed healing ointment on my head. I am healed, restored and set free because of you, my beloved Father, Amen.*

Now go and write down these words. Write them in a book. They will stand until the end of time as a witness.

— *ISAIAH 30:8 NLT*

CONTENTS

ACKNOWLEDGMENTS

Appreciation is a wonderful thing. It makes what is excellent in others belong to us as well. [1]

— VOLTAIRE

To my precious husband Greg, I thank you for being so extremely patient with me, for supporting me as I sold out to be the absolute Jesus freak I have become and always believing in all of me. I appreciate you allowing me so much time in the driver's seat while I stopped to capture images of God along the way (and for enduring my sudden brake checks). Second, to God, I love you the most.

To my treasured boys Owen and McCrae, you both forever changed my world and the point of my compass the day each of you were born. The Word of God says the Lord God formed man of dust from the ground and breathed into his nostrils the breath of life and man became. Thank you beautiful children of God for giving me life and purpose on earth as your mom. I love you both to the ends of the earth and into eternity.

To my Spiritual parents, Jack and Peggy McBride. Thank you for your fervent prayers over me and my precious family. For breathing wisdom over me while providing instruction and correction. Above all, thank you for believing in me. You are so precious and deeply loved.

To my Spiritual mentor, Debbie Hudspeth, thank you for calling me out of the desert and launching me into position for God's Kingdom. You have sown many seeds into my life and have been obedient in the process of watering. I am forever grateful for the words God has delivered through you. To the daughter of King Jesus, I love you sister.

To my Pastor, our church families, Lifegroup members, Bible study group, ministries and clients, thank you for every opportunity to sit under your teachings. Privileged to have encountered some amazing people who I proudly call family and friends in Christ. Forever more grateful for your prayers, words of encouragement and faithful fellowship in my life.

To my beautiful friend and soul sister in Christ Courtney McEwen. When I was unsure of the process, God sent me you. Thank you for reading my stories and then placing your fingerprints upon these pages. You have inspired me in so many ways, I cannot record them all. I thank you and I love you, my sister in Christ.

To my dear friend and Monday morning self-care sister Chris Fenoglio. In the past five years you have heard my many testimonies week after week. You have laughed and cried with me. You have even dried my tears with your endless supply of tissue. Thank you for lending me your ear and praying me through the tears. The time you took to read each story and connect my thoughts to the dot is beyond return. I thank you for your Scripture truth, your wisdom and support. To you much love is deserved, my forever sister in Christ.

To my dear friend, client, tech guy and gifted grammar saint Kevin Corado. Thank you for your constant support and for being my tech support all these years. You have heard my many dreams, visions, stories and testimonies of God and held them close to heart. You have been a voice of accountability over this book. When the voice of uncertainty to get these pages printed out, your line rang loud, and you answered always.

It was you who assured me there is still a way. Thank you for believing in me always. Much Love owed to you!

INTRODUCTION

Writing is the painting of the voice.[1]

— VOLTAIRE

Years ago, I began to seek the heart of my Abba Father in a very purposeful way. I awoke each morning much different than in years before. I started the day asking God for new vision, eyes that were wide open to the revelation awaiting in each new day. I asked God to retrace my steps in life, illuminating anything I might have previously missed. I had a deep desire to see things from God's perspective, with a pure heart and clear sight. God's word in Psalm 51:10 (NLT) says: Create in me a clean heart, O God. Renew a loyal spirit within me. The more mornings I cried out rehearing the lines of this Scripture, the more God's beauty was revealed through my windshield. Scripture tells us: "God conceals the revelation of his word in the hiding place of his glory. But the honor of kings is revealed by how they thoroughly search out the deeper meaning of all that God says" (Proverbs 25:2 TPT).

If I was going to make understanding of what the depths of this verse meant, I had to find privilege in my daily obedience. Indeed, it was time to receive my gift of kingship that was provided to me because of God's grace and the redeeming blood of Christ.

As you begin in our daily journey over the next one hundred days, read this devotional book knowing my prayer for each hand that turns the pages has the gift of kingship buried within. Over, and over again His mercies are new every day. God waits to be invited. Always willing to help you discover His fresh outlook into your seconds, minutes, hours, days, weeks, months, years and moments. Let your hearts be stirred and what lays dormant come to life as you discover the absolute privilege you have as kings in the Kingdom of God.

May you meet with the Creator of the heavens and earth with surrendered hearts, seeking to discover more about Him in the stillness of your days. In King Jesus' Mighty Name, Amen.

WALK OUT OF THE FLESH

DAY 1

For we are not fighting against flesh-and-blood enemies, but against evil rulers and authorities of the unseen world, against mighty powers in this dark world, and against evil spirits in the heavenly places.

— EPHESIANS 6:12 NLT

I remember a time, not long ago, when I fought everyday life from a fleshly perspective. I entered a season of life where the Lord had some dealings with me on many matters dealing with my heart. Finding myself wrestling in a real-life battle with someone I once thought to be more like a mother figure in my life had awoken something in me. Although at the time I thought I had every tool I needed to deploy against the enemy I was surely missing the main weapon. It was not long into the battle before the Lord showed me what was missing from my she-shed: The Written Word.

We are to walk with this understanding in mind, we are made up of three-part beings. We are spirit, we have a soul, and we all live in a body. Our bodies are born into a sinful world. We are born carriers to the true analogy of a dog-eat-dog world. Our bodies are full of functions and we maneuver life through our bodies processing the physical world with our brains and senses. Our souls are responsible for our personality format. If anyone ever preached to you about your mind, will and emotions then this is where those things take up residence. There is the conscious side and the sub-conscious side that function here. The conscious does our reasoning and thinking. The subconscious is responsible for belief, attitude, feelings, emotions and memories. Our will is what gives us the green light to make choices. Now we approach the good part. Our spirit or some say our spirit man! This is the sole purpose of life. This is the area that is visited through the gift of the Holy Spirit when you give your life over to Christ. Our spirit will have a conscience between what is right and what is wrong through the gift of receiving the Holy Spirit.

It is in our spiritual health we will find great significance in enriching our emotional state which in return will influence our physical health. Have you ever seen someone glow differently after walking with God for some time? This is where the illumination is coming from, changed from the inside out. We must learn to not become conductors to what our emotions instruct our flesh to do. Spending ample amount of time with God in His word will bring on an illumination. The same goes for spending time in the world; it will bring on its own set of emotions or lack thereof.

The true enemy lies in the unseen realm (spiritual realm) digging up our past and creating spiritual evilness (amongst one another we struggle to foresee). What we choose to not heal from will eventually bleed onto others and down to future bloodlines in generations to come. If we search Scripture, we will find that Christ has all authority over that realm. Rest assured your weapon is "The Word of God". Let us pick it up and get the work started! Join me in the next ninety-nine days as I lead you into my own personal experiences with *A Gospel Encounter*.

FINAL WORD: May this prayer be spoken over you, let the fight begin from Victory not for Victory, Amen.

SURRENDER

DAY 2

Yet if you devote your heart to him and stretch out your hands to him, if you put away the sin that is in your hand and allow no evil to dwell in your tent, then, free of fault, you will lift up your face; you will stand firm and without fear.

— *JOB 11:13-15 NIV*

I n 2017 I remember it just like yesterday. It was fall and I had been preparing for our first ever annual ladies conference themed "Surrender" held at the local church we attended. The wind was blowing, and I had needed to head to town to gather some things. As I exited the front gates of our property and prepared to get out of the vehicle to close the gate a red-tail hawk had flown by my driver's side window and landed directly in front of the vehicle on a T-post. Now if you are familiar with T-post, it is a fancy terminology for poles in the country to hold fences up. Take note they truly bare little room for much of a ledge. I quickly grabbed my camera phone and began videoing and capturing a few shots. In my spirit, I felt this sudden urgency to not stop the video.

What felt like ten minutes was only really three minutes or so as the wind blew the red tail hawk gently about. I watched as the hawk grasped firmer to the T-post, bracing against the wind. When it could no longer stand the weight of the wind it took flight. Just as it freed itself in midair, I caught what looked like a cloud of smoke following its tail feathers. After reviewing this magnificent video several thousand times, I was fully convinced. My Heavenly Father was all about showing me an image of true surrender. Many times we take the weight of what was never ours to begin with. We cling, clench and grasp onto it for dear life. It is not until we have reached exhaustion that we choose surrender. Only then in that place can God move in and make a way with what was always His way to begin with. God's sooner is so much better than your later!

FINAL WORD: I have prayed for you to go ahead and lay it down at the feet of Jesus, Amen.

HELP IS ON ITS WAY

DAY 3

*But when the Father sends the Advocate as my representative – that is,
the Holy Spirit – he will teach you everything and will remind you of
everything I have told you.*

— *JOHN 14:26 NLT*

Owning a business of my own had frequented my
dreams. When the opportunity revealed itself
to move not just my career home but business
too, I rejoiced. Being more available to my children and
my husband topped my prayer list. When the door
opened, we walked through it. On a particular spring day
while in my shop, I had taken a later appointment than
usual. My client and I had both noticed a scissortail bird
resting on the barbwire fence out my shop window.
Making small talk we noticed a dryer sheet hung on the
fence. Continuing to monitor the bird's actions in the
window, it would try fervently to yank the dryer sheet off
by scratching its beak across it. This behavior continued
again and again with no luck freeing the dryer sheet. I

said aloud with a slight giggle to my client "Hold on please, help is on its way". Stepping out briefly, I made a few adjustments to help the dryer sheet untangle. Stepping back into the shop, patiently waiting for the return of the bird, which by the way, never appeared again. Later that evening as I closed shop up, I had walked my kids over to the fence where this dryer sheet still rested. I shared the story of the bird with them and let them in on a little secret, God was showing us an example of "Help is on its way".

The next morning came and it was Saturday. My husband and boys awoke early to take care of animals. As they went out that morning I stayed behind in the house. Short minutes later I confirmed the previous day's encounter with the dryer sheet and the bird. The neighbor's bull had gotten out. My husband decided to push it back to its home on foot while the boys took the farm truck and followed behind at a distance. The bull had decided "not today," did a turn back, and trampled over my husband, repeatedly driving and stomping him into the ground. Our two young boys were left in the vehicle to witness this scene.

With a decision at hand help was now on the way. Our older son behind the wheel punched the gas and came to a sudden stop watching the bull leap back over the fence. The bull unharmed and my husband with a truck tire now resting inches from his head, a little trampled and bruised but alive. This day would forever enlist our family to God prompting a message delivered in the previous day "Help is on its way". Is there a message you are certain God has delivered in your inbox that may need to be opened?

·   ·   ·

FINAL WORD: My prayer is for all to know The Holy Spirit as not only your helper but as your comforter, Amen.

I BELIEVE WHAT YOU SAY TO ME

DAY 4

But the LORD said to Samuel, "Don't judge by his appearance or height, for I have rejected him. The LORD doesn't see things the way you see them. People judge by outward appearance, but the LORD looks at the heart."

— *1 SAMUEL 16:7 NLT*

Remarkably, year after year on our place we have shared in the opportunity to watch life reproduce through our momma cows. Each year we have a fresh herd of new babies. It is an extremely exciting time of year. We love watching the babies venture down to the watering hole on our place and learn the process of summer cool down. The mommas standing high above them on the banks, at close distance, watching with such intent. The babies stepping in hoof deep and then taking a running pass into the shallow waters, then swiftly return to the mother's touch. Several times I have thought to myself these babies have these incredible moms who not only believe in them but whisper through silence, repeated looks of encouragement over them. Again, and again, the beautiful thing I am reminded of is that the babies believe the looks given too. How often do you question what God says to you?

Having many opportunities throughout the years to practice and "believe what He has said to me", I still go cold from time to time. Many of us could probably agree to some degree on this statement. We often confuse His words with the words of the enemy. Now do not miss this, a real-live enemy is wanting to prowl in on all matters especially any that build God's Kingdom. There have been several times where I would attend an atmosphere pouring out God's word, and catch myself thinking "How do you know it was God?" This recurring question would also frequently hit the top ten questions and answers panel. Just like the panel's responses to this question, I agree and learn from encounters with God.

The God encounters will only be found in the acts of obedience. God's voice will never condemn you. The enemy condemns you. God is Love so there is nothing you could do for Him to make Him love you less or more. God just simply loves all of you. If by chance you have missed an act of obedience, guess what? God still loves you! If He has asked you to do something for Him and you did not believe it was Him, it is okay. God is a great Father and just like a father He will ask you again. God knows you so very well, He also knows all the ways to ask you. God even knows all the unique ways you may need to see Him, hear Him or feel Him to believe that it was in fact Him. God is not shocked, not surprised nor caught off guard by a thing. Keep stepping out, keep believing Him for your next, and remember there will always come a next!

. . .

FINAL WORD: My prayer that you come to know God as He already has come for you, that you understand how much He loves you and for eternity He believes in you, Amen.

GOD IS IN THE DETAILS

DAY 5

In the beginning God created the heavens and the earth. The earth was formless and empty, and darkness covered the deep waters. And the Spirit of God was hovering over the surface of the waters.

— GENESIS 1:1-2 NLT

In mid-February of 2018, winter had set in and was leaving its mark in North Texas. No one had an idea that it was going to get that cold or produce that much ice in our county. Many of us went some time without power. The power companies seemed to work around the clock trying to melt the layers of ice upon power lines and clean up tree limbs that could no longer bear the weight of the ice. Walking outside I was just mesmerized by the winter wonderland before my eyes. Grabbing my camera I began walking our property asking God to direct my steps to the next picture. There was so much beauty it began to feel a bit overwhelming. To capture it all was an endless storyline. As I walked and photographed, step after step I continued to hear a repeated sound from God, saying in my spirit "I am in the details". In response I sounded off back to the Father "you sure are." Amazingly enough I took notice of the details trying not to leave any out. Not one piece of our property went uncovered from the detail of God. God, the Creator of All, formed a blanket of snow and ice to fall over His creation. That week, leaving not one thing uncovered, God was sure to cover the land. God is famous for being extremely detail oriented and even you, my friend, were formed with every intricate detail already in His mind. Around every corner God has stamped His claim. Can you see it now or will you open your eyes to look for it?

FINAL WORD: I pray an extension of your sights beyond what is in front of you and a supernatural finding of God in all creation, Amen.

LORD YOUR SERVANT IS LISTENING

DAY 6

So he said to Samuel, "Go and lie down again, and if someone calls again, say, 'Speak, LORD, your servant is listening.'" So Samuel went back to bed.

— *1 SAMUEL 3:9 NLT*

In the book of 1 Samuel 3, this young boy Samuel served the Lord by assisting a very old and almost blind priest named, Eli. As Samuel would fall fast asleep, he would hear his name being called. Samuel again and again would get up and run to Eli saying, "Here I am". Eli responded stating "I did not call you son." This continued in a pattern for two more times. By now Eli realized that the Lord was calling on the boy. Samuel had not had a relationship with God yet. Eli instructed the young boy Samuel if it happens again respond by saying, "Speak, LORD, your servant is listening".

I love to share that I have always had horses around in my life since birth. Both parents and grandparents loved the horse and all it stood for. I should probably say that I do not remember a time in my life not having horses. Out of all God's beautiful creatures, I believe that horses rank at the top of His priority list. I like to also believe that the horse had an extra measure of God's handy touch in having it all together. There are times when I gaze at the horse finding myself enthralled by their appearance and movement. Years of being in the company of the horse, I have learned that they are a very responsive animal. The horse will pour out absolutely all you ask of it over and over again. They will condition themselves to a routine and soul tie with owners or stable mates. The horse is accustomed to the patterns you put in place and the demands thrown upon them. A whistle, clap or the shaking of a grain can from across the pasture and the horse generally will respond.

The horse and rider have such a reciprocal kinship. The voice of God works similarly in the relationship described here with the horse. God chooses to call out to us sometimes over and over again and we have the free will to choose to respond. God may even choose to use a stable mate (someone or someone's) in your life drawing you to the feed trough. God waits patiently for His children called by name to respond. Do you have a "Speak, Lord your servant is listening" in your Spirit today?

FINAL WORD: I pray for your ears to be opened, and your response time be swift to the One calling you to the feed trough, Amen.

YOU HAVE A FRIEND IN ME

DAY 7

I no longer call you slaves, because a master doesn't confide in his slaves. Now you are my friends, since I have told you everything the Father told me.

— *JOHN 15:15 NLT*

When my husband and I ventured out and bought our new home a handful of years ago we knew at some point we would need cattle on our place. Neither one of us were much prepared financially to purchase any after just buying the place. We began to pray and even create a vision board of things we would love to see God do for us with our new place. It was not very long after pinning a black and white picture to our vision board of a cow, we swiftly saw the opportunity of God moving on behalf of our prayers. We had a local in the area step in and offer us opportunity to run cattle on our place. In exchange for the grazing land the cattle would be taken care of and all their needs met. My husband and I accepted this offer with full vision that God moved through our prayers on our behalf. This arrangement went on for a few years. During the time our family grew as close to the cows as we did with the man. Our family would watch and care for daily needs and receive extended invitations to help with other cattle. My husband and I would put a little aside monthly still praying and believing that we would someday have our own herd or the chance to buy perhaps a few of these.

In the third year, we had approached our newfound friend about purchasing the cows and babies currently cared for on our place. Graciously accepting our offer, the once spoken prayer now offered us possession and ownership. But God, did not just stop there. Our new friend had ties to a bull and had offered to help us grow what was now our current herd in the coming year. Again, a unique opportunity presented itself for our family's benefits.

Placing emphasis on our visions not only allows growth in our prayer life, it offered a place for God to share His lines of communication reminding us of what He can do. God moves on behalf of His children's prayers. For not one moment have we missed that God has an established hand on all. Envision all this stemming from one black and white cow picture pinned to a vision board. Even a shred of paper can become no small task for God to move on your behalf, reminding you to look beyond that and you will find much more than a friend in God!

FINAL WORD: My prayer encourages you to allow yourself to express your needs and let them be known to God, that you take great opportunities in expressing your desires and that you sit back to watch the kind of God moving on your behalf, Amen.

CONSIDER AN UPGRADE

DAY 8

Don't you realize that your body is the temple of the Holy Spirit, who lives in you and was given to you by God? You do not belong to yourself, for God bought you with a high price. So you must honor God with your body.

— *1 CORINTHIANS 6:19-20 NLT*

The young teenage girl I speak of was me often looking out upon the peers around me and desiring the likeness of their hair, makeup, and even clothing. Being that girl was so extremely tormenting. Every morning before school thinking about what was I going to wear and did it reveal enough? I would spend extra time in the bathroom making sure all the lumps and bumps were out of my slicked-back ponytail, braid or bun. I would put on makeup heavy only to mask my own identity.

It was when I became a mother to my precious boys that I really grasped the concept of what it was I had been doing all those years. As a new mother, something took root, the hostage of identity began to change in me. Appearance began to not feel like my own anymore. Not talking about the messy hair do not care or the sweatpants wardrobe for every occasion either. I began to believe and understand whose temple I was placed in and finding comfort in the skin I was in became forefront. Peace washed over me with a clean face, and no makeup mask required. I was now the student to a teacher (Holy Spirit) who was revealing to me on what a mother should model. Motherhood was a welcome home celebration to do its best work in me. Have little ones they all said, but little ones will suck the life out of you said no one ever!

Makeup, hair and good dress attire would take a complete backseat to motherhood. What had happened to me in the process is best explained like this: you know how cars, trucks, SUV's and mini vans come in different size, shapes and models. You may have your XL plain strip down model, maybe your XLT with a few bells and whistles then you have your Lariat, King Ranch and Platinum models that typically come with much more than just the bells and whistles.

Well, I relate these car packages to the process God takes us through as we begin to make room for Him in our identity walk. It is your free will to allow Him to make the upgrade in you. You cannot be all the bells and whistles all the time. At some point every upgrade you have grown accustomed to will cost you. Eventually whether it be motherhood or whatever this life has in store for you personally. There comes a point of understanding that we all draw near to, that our bodies do not belong to us after all. Offer up to God the stripped-down version of yourself then watch Him add all the bells and whistles making you upgraded.

. . .

FINAL WORD: I pray that you allow God to take you from the stripped-down version to the very best version He has for you. Allow a signed contract in your heart for the comforter to complete the upgrades, Amen.

IF IT DOES NOT OPEN IT IS NOT YOUR DOOR

DAY 9

I tell you, you can pray for anything, and if you believe that you've received it, it will be yours.

— *MARK 11:24 NLT*

Over two years ago my husband and I had started praying for God to open yet another opportunity for my small business to move home. One day he had stopped by my shop that was then at the time in town and asked me if I wanted to head to lunch. I accepted the invitation and he had decided to take me to look at portable storage buildings. The time was around late August. We patiently walked through them on the lot and dreamed of what we could do with designing it as a hair salon. The owner of the buildings kindly stepped away and allowed us the time to dream up blueprints in our minds. Before leaving that day my husband and I stood face to face holding one another's hand and we prayed, "God if this is your will send a sign and let every door swing open that no man can shut in Jesus' Name." We then walked out believing that this building was ours next and that God would make it known very soon, as He had for us so many times before.

Well, you probably can guess how the story ended. It was about one month later, and God revealed the open doors. The doors would not only swing wide open for this opportunity to have my hair salon at home, but in the matter of three short months the entire thing was completed. God would send every resource, material and labor hand needed to complete the construction of this building. I remember my husband, kids and I working long days and then coming home and still having enough energy to complete the task before us. Every day we stepped foot into the building we saw God move again. On the final completion day as our little family gathered, we sat on the floor, holding hands in a circle like young school age kids. One by one we praised and prayed out loud to God who opened every door without us having the need to push, pull or kick. I share this with you now. If it is your door, God will meet you in the place of resistance. All you will need to do is get up and walk on through.

FINAL WORD: My prayer is while you ask for it, you come into agreement with it that it is yours, Amen.

GREAT IS YOUR FAITHFULNESS

DAY 10

Great is his faithfulness; his mercies begin afresh each morning.

— *LAMENTATIONS 3:23 NLT*

How often do we question God's faithfulness? Throughout the Bible, we can find story after story where God's faithfulness had always been. So why is it that we find ourselves up against this question time and time again? I believe that we have become a generation focused on a quick fix mentality. We spend our days wrapped in the many resources right at our fingertips. My children say to me all the time "Mom we do not need Google when we have God right?" That is right, the Word of God is google.

When we go to the doctor's office, we expect them to diagnose us and give a quick fix. Most times that can be found in medications while trial and erroring until something finally helps. Now we can even go to the internet for just about anything without even having to believe God for a single thing. We get sick, there is a pill for that.

We want to shed a few pounds, there is a different pill or surgery for that too. We want to remove a wrinkle or two or three, well there is a simple night cream for that or then again surgery. We want nicer things we cannot afford, well there is a way to finance that. We have all the right quick fix tips at our disposal. I share these few points with you because I too have taken part of the quick fixes on many areas I just discussed throughout my own life. I believe that where I have experienced God's faithfulness in abundance has been in the simple obedience of waiting and trusting God. My newest approach is to take time and invite God into every decision each day. God leans in with full understanding of each day and outcome of all moments I am approaching ahead. Allowing God, the opportunity in, acknowledges His faithful works in the end. With inviting Him in, all I want God to know is that I care about what He has to say about my day, every day.

Think about your marriage or a relationship in general for a moment. If you had a conflict of some sort that needed resolution, would you not seek the advice and comfort of a trusted one or of your spouse? So why would you not allow the One who knows you better than anyone else the opportunity to try to be the solution? We have all at one point or another experienced the faithfulness of God in our lives. Cling onto those moments of hope and reject the urge to go on without God's help and guidance.

FINAL WORD: I pray a word of encouragement over you to not allow the tendencies of the flesh to rise and override your current circumstance of hope. Forge your faith where the movement of God's faithfulness has revealed itself many times before, Amen.

LET THE DEAD THINGS GO

DAY 11

He cuts off every branch of mine that doesn't produce fruit, and he prunes the branches that do bear fruit so they will produce even more.

— JOHN 15:2 NLT

There was a quote I once read from an unknown source that said, "The trees can show us the importance of letting the dead things go".[1] I often thought of this quote come fall when all the beautiful colors are revealed and the trees shed all their leaves, most of the time leaving a little mess for us to clean up.

Now I live in the country and my property has many trees in a few isolated areas. I have watched them now for a few years. The changing of the leaves begins about the first part of October around our place and then by the end of October, the leaves are falling with absolutely no assistance from me. Usually, before spring my husband, kids and I will head out to prune the large trees. My boys and I stand positioned on the ground patiently waiting on the first branch to be cut off by my husband, chainsaw in hand. It is the job of my children and me to load the branches as my husband is the pruner. The process of tree trimming takes the cooperation of all of us and the obedience of our own work of hands. Can trees care for themselves? Yes, and many do in the deep forests. For the tree to reach their full potential in life the process of pruning is a much needed process.

I love what John tells us in verse 15:2, God the true vine teaches us about the pruning process that must occur to our branches. Just like the tree needs our assistance in removing some of the dead branches to reach life's fullest potential, we must be cared for in the same manner in order to reach a place of fruitfulness. As we continue to be fruitful branches, we still need cutting or perhaps just pruning here and there. All of this is done by the work of God for our own growth and best potential. If our choice is to live apart from God, then alone we are the caretaker of nothing more than an infectious overgrowth contaminating the forest. This is not only detrimental to ourselves, but potentially affecting others in our part of the forest. We all need God and His pruning assistance to help us produce a strong, healthy forest. Learn to let all the dead things go and join in the building of a fruitful forest.

FINAL WORD: I pray for you to endure the pruning of your branches so you can continue to receive a fruitful life, giving you a connection to the One and only vine for eternity, Amen.

THE ROAD LESS TRAVELED

DAY 12

You can enter God's Kingdom only through the narrow gate. The highway to hell is broad, and its gate is wide for the many who choose that way. But the gateway to life is very narrow and the road is difficult, and only a few ever find it.

— *MATTHEW 7:13-14 NLT*

L ooking back over the years I had always thought that when I surrendered my life to Christ, well that was it! I am good and I am in. Really, I did not need to do anything more but admit that I was a sinner and ask for forgiveness, believing that Christ died for my sins and rose again. Now I would turn from my sins and accept Christ in my heart and my life, committed to trusting and following Christ as my Lord and Savior. Might I add that I would need to show up for church now and again too!

After attending church for some time, I would hear my Pastor preach on the importance of the narrow gate. I became inspired to study the importance of this narrow gate. The narrow gate represents our decision to follow Jesus. The wide gate is a decision to not follow Jesus and continue the path of the wide highway to hell. Most of us can say, at least if you are reading this far, that we all have at some point given our lives to Christ or we may be considering even now to do so. Going to church is a part of what we as Christians do, we might even consider that to be just enough. I am here to say I thought the same for many years too. It was not until I started to reach out from a place of hunger, that I craved more of Jesus in other areas of my everyday walk.

Now reading the word I began to identify with what my friend Matthew was saying about the narrow gate in my own life. I share with you that if and even when you begin to share Jesus in every single part of your life, not limited to your workplace, children's sports, school functions or just simply in your weekly Walmart trips, you too will begin to take note of those not yet walking through the narrow gate.

It may surprise you at first like it did me and even my children. In regard to my children, God has always been a firsthand experience to them. They were given the opportunity to celebrate him through walking in the shadows of our obedience.

Sharing Jesus as a family everywhere, our children are hardwired to notice anyone who may not know Jesus. Someone may not know Jesus or was never afforded the opportunity to meet Jesus in their childhood years but this does not disqualify anyone the same opportunity. I encourage you to share Jesus anywhere and everywhere, in any way you can. Through your simple act of obedience, they may feel qualified to take the walk through the narrow gate.

FINAL WORD: My prayer is for you to feel qualified to walk with me through the narrow gate, Amen.

HALLELUJAH

DAY 13

Hallelujah! Praise the Lord! How beautiful it is when we sing our praises to the beautiful God, for praise makes you lovely before him and brings him great delight! The Lord builds up Jerusalem; he gathers up the outcasts and brings them home. He heals the wounds of every shattered heart. He sets his stars in place, calling them all by their names. How great is our God! There's absolutely nothing his power cannot accomplish, and he has infinite understanding of everything.

— *PSALM 147:1-5 TPT*

Growing up from time to time I had heard this phrase chanted: "Hallelujah, Praise the Lord!" At school kids would say it if something great was happening or maybe just if something went the way someone planned or wished for. At this point in my life I'm not sure I can even recall anyone ever releasing a Hallelujah over the bad they may have been going through. Can you relate?

When I stumbled upon this verse in The Passion Translation, I could not help but to rejoice over the words written before me. I could not just stop at the opening verse of Psalm 147 because it explained so much more in great detail taking place throughout the first five verses.

I think the human side of me is programmed in a cycle of rejoicing over only the good coming my way. As I am moved beyond the good, I must also include the days that are not so good. Why do I find it hard to praise on the bad days? What do I praise God for? Hear what this verse is saying, "For praise makes you lovely before him and brings him great delight!" God is not trapped nor limited to the circumstances of today only, that is not of great importance to Him. In all the good, the bad, the ugly of the day none of it holds a candle to the voice of your praise. That is what delights Him most. The next verse tells us, "He gathers up the outcasts and brings them home." Is home not a place that you find rest in and shelter from the outside. A good day is coming home, Hallelujah Praise the Lord! A great day is knowing that He heals wounds past, present and future because there is absolutely nothing His power cannot accomplish. And even if by our standards it is a bad day, God has a place and name for all stars in the skies and He surely has an infinite understanding of your entire day as well. All your needs, good, bad, ugly or indifferent, God wants to meet you with His already accomplished power. God wants your everlasting Hallelujah!

FINAL WORD: I pray you continue to raise your Hallelujah no matter the peaks of your mountains and the depths of your valleys, Amen.

SWEETER THAN HONEY

DAY 14

The rarest treasures of life are found in his truth. That's why I prize God's word like others prize the finest gold. Nothing brings the soul such sweetness as seeking his living words.

— PSALM 19:10 TPT

What happens when your thought process comes into contact with God's commandments and instructions? Do you know the God who speaks throughout the Bible? Do you see His word as shackles over your life or the key that freed the shackles? Beloved friend, for so many years as I read God's word and even heard it preached, I would fight the feeling of imprisonment. My own set of daily standards collided with what I thought to be God needing some sort of checklist. It was not until I realized that God's instructions were never written to become a set of boxes to checkmark. At the end of my days God would not be a clipboard kind of God. He was not buying in bulk highlighters from the things I did not accomplish either. His instructions were set forth as a roadmap because, guess what? Not one of us could or ever would walk in perfection.

The instructions would become commandments to walk out of the shackles my friends. There is never a need for a checklist, nor a need to have it all checked off either. That was the standard set in the Old Testament and God wanted us to come in contact with His new ways. He wanted to be sure that the book we would someday read was not all talk. God wanted a walk that would elevate us from the talker to the walker.

The Word of God was not meant as a conversation piece. It was meant for those who did more walking than talking. God went ahead and walked out the extra mile that we would not be able to withstand and did what only one God could do. He sent His One and only Son to talk the talk and walk the walk. God sent us His One and only Son that proved that all the things on this earth that we will ever endure or encounter had been done already.

Each one of us, every single day, are walking through something. The beauty you should hear in it is this: we can pick up the Bible, thumb through a few pages and find a story of not only the One, but many someones who had walked through something similar to our situation. The fact is that Jesus walked through it all for you, for me, and for many still yet to come. And if we choose to believe even bigger than that, we could understand that Jesus is walking through it with us at this very moment right now. The commandments, the instructions, they were never intended to shackle us to our circumstances or imprison us to attempt perfection. They were designed as a blueprint to bring revival and joy to the heart. Insight to our situation. A warning at times. A

**reward for our perseverance, and last, to SET THE
CAPTIVE FREE!**

*FINAL WORD: I pray the treasures of truth become your blueprint and
that you desire the sweetness through digging out all truth in God's living
word, Amen.*

CLEARED VESSEL

DAY 15

In a wealthy home some utensils are made of gold and silver, and some are made of wood and clay. The expensive utensils are used for special occasions, and the cheap ones are for everyday use. If you keep yourself pure, you will be a special utensil for honorable use. Your life will be clean, and you will be ready for the Master to use you for every good work.

— *2 TIMOTHY 2:20-21 NLT*

The growing childhood memories of holidays. In our home we celebrated and gathered for Thanksgiving, Christmas and New Year's. I never put much thought into the things that seemed to come together so effortlessly during these holidays every year. Until I started caring for my own home and family. I remember gathering in one home in the earlier afternoons. The men gathered around watching sports on the television, keeping in perfect rhythm with conversation. The women prepping the table and meal. Before us was a lavish table set with fine china that only made its seasonal debut for this time of year.

Most all year the china could be adored in a large hutch that glistened from the previous day's lemon Pledge film layers. The plates ever so gently removed and placed at the adult table, then the bowls, the silverware, the napkins and last the glasses. Today I can still remember the sound of the cracking of ice removed from plastic trays and the ting of the glasses as we placed three square ice cubes in each. Memories like these take me way back.

When I think of the beautiful hutch filled with the beautiful dishes awaiting their season to be used, I am reminded of the kind of person I want to be. I believe God is looking for that someone to use every day. I want to be that person that is pure, that is polished, that is clean, that is sparkling, ready to be assigned for God's best dinner setting. I want to be ready, the one invited to God's table at any given moment's notice. What story are you waiting on to be written before you really think it is you God can use?

FINAL WORD: I pray that you become recognized as a polished utensil ready to be used in the hand of our mighty God, Amen.

WHAT IF?

DAY 16

But those who trust in the LORD will find new strength. They will soar high on wings like eagles. They will run and not grow weary. They will walk and not faint.

— *ISAIAH 40:31 NLT*

One of my favorite quotes written by Erin Hanson goes like this "What if I fall?" "Oh, but my darling, what if you fly?"[1] There is something to be said for all those whose trust is in the Lord. I cannot say that my level of trust in the Lord has always been something to write home about. Not even the smallest consideration of trust would have a presence in my every day walk until over a handful of years ago. The younger version would tell you that much of my distrust stemmed from childhood insecurities. Home life paints a big picture into what our level of confidence will be in the future.

Forming from my earliest childhood memories, the constant debates and arguments about money were the sounds that echoed inside the walls of home. The best explanation is, when things were good, they were good, but when things were bad, they were so very bad. Later in life things were revealed to be worse than any portion of good. This is when I became an insecure, displaced, childlike product of divorced parents.

Many, many, many years later the man who helped father me met with me for a heartfelt conversation that led somewhere. Walking away from that discussion left me with this conclusion: to follow the world and fill your-selves with all it has to offer in the end only leads to endless weariness. What could it be that we are missing?

The longing we all desire for is to be loved, to be found, and to be accepted. The things that help separate us farther from that is the world and what it provides. All sorts of temporary fillers. God is the fix, and He is the love that you have longed for, putting a stop to the void. God has never been lost, it was I who was lost, using up every ounce of the world to fill that longing desire of want. God was still the One to be trusted in finding me at all costs. God never stopped in pursuit of you or me, even when all the things of the world may or may not have been there.

His children have always been His point of passion. It is God that accepts you whenever and however you are. It is you who must regain the trust and choose to accept Him back. When the resources of this world are diminished, taking a back seat to what only God can accomplish, the trust is only then restored. It has never been easy for anyone to fly away from the things of the world, but what is found following these things will only cause us to fall and fail. Your flight pattern with God awaits you.

. . .

FINAL WORD: I pray for you to let loose in meeting with the world to draw strength and invite you in to gather your strength from the One supplier who will never deplete you, Amen.

BEAUTY IN THE SILENCE

DAY 17

*And yet, "Better to have one handful with quietness than two handfuls
with hard work and chasing the wind."*

— *ECCLESIASTES 4:6 NLT*

What I am about to share is not to discredit a time and place for hard work. I believe God at times helps us to be reminded that hard work is not our sole purpose here on earth. Rather the line of work we are in is God's Kingdom-building process, bringing us into a platform He can be glorified in. I have an amazingly gifted, hardworking husband that loves nothing more than to see his family provided for and for that I am certainly grateful. In his career, he is required to be available twenty-four hours a day, seven days a week, three hundred sixty-five days a year. With that said, I would like you to be reminded that God is a twenty-four hour a day, seven days a week, three hundred sixty-five days a year on-call God.

Sometimes, life gets us caught up in our daily regimens and careers, leading us to forget that you can never out work or out-give what God already has done. During this book-writing process, God not only reminded our family of this, but He gave us a small demonstration. If my husband was available for that type of workload then God was surely going to clock him in for His use.

In the middle of the night recently, my husband had woken me from a dead sleep holding his chest saying, "Get me to the ER, I think I may be having a heart attack." The minutes, the speedometer and passing cars could not move fast enough in that thirty-minute car ride. My two young boys and myself praying aloud, crying out to God, pleading the blood of Jesus over my husband, praying bouncing prayers one after another, taking turns the entire car ride. Praise God, we arrived and were able to get him in the emergency room still alive and breathing. It all turned out he was not having a heart attack after all. Instead, ruptured ulcers. Nonetheless, it was still scary for our family and now looking back even more so for him. As my husband's three-day hospital stay transpired, it appeared perhaps God needed him for something much bigger.

My husband had shared with me briefly after leaving the hospital something that happened within that suite. One evening as I had left for a few hours to tend to our children, one of the nurses had come to him and asked: "What is the secret to your marriage?" While tending to my husband's needs the nurse had shared some personal relationship struggles and was looking for some sort of words or encouragement. In response to her question my husband shared with her that twenty years together had not always been easy. That in twenty years we chose a lot of things to do on our own. As you walk out marriage you will find many weak spots that were not present in the beginning. The best advice I can give you and that I have ever done for myself, our marriage, and our family, always put God front and center. My husband explained that without Him your foundation is weak. Had it been possible that my husband became a little busy clocking in to be reminded of this? The answer to that we may never know. But for now, we will praise Him for His gentle reminder. When you become available to God, awaken each day to clock in to serve God. He may be required to send you a friendly reminder every now and again as needed.

> Never underestimate the power of silence. Some of the most profound insights come from the quietest of places.[1]
>
> — *AUTHOR UNKNOWN*

FINAL WORD: Be prayerful that in the busiest times of your schedule God can still clock you in, Amen.

COMPARISON

DAY 18

So may we never be arrogant, or look down on another, for each of us is an original. We must forsake all jealousy that diminishes the value of others.

— *GALATIANS 5:26 TPT*

Recently I heard someone share something like what I am going to share with you today. Like it was at the time for me, I pray that you put this token in your back pocket and run with it. Our twenties, oh my, my, our twenties. What a time in our life where we look to who is around us and become the crowd-pleasers. Let us visualize our suitcases on this journey while we travel our timeline together.

Our suitcases in life at that time are small things most of us just moved out from home, yet we somehow figure out how to overfill them. Well, we certainly are not at all worried that it ends up overfilled and we try to return with more than we came with. Young and inexperienced with travel we will just consider buying another and over filling that one too before the trip ends. We find ourselves closing in on the end of our twenties trip and at that point have acquired many trinkets. We must leave with it all and get our many treasures home and acquired for others to simply rave over.

It is now our thirties. Oh wow, looking around our circle of friends they all now have husbands, homes, cars and kids they are traveling with. Don't you think it is time? We need the husband, the wedding, it must be bliss. The home, the fenced in yard for the kids of course and the car. Do not forget the midsize car! Wait, do not forget all my old suitcases please and yes, I will need them all. Wait they do not fit. I think I may need to get some help downsizing. Calling in reinforcements to help remove a suitcase here and there. Purchasing a slightly larger midsize, one should do for now. There, finally, at last, room has been made for what is coming in the months ahead. A midsize suitcase will do, I did catch a glimpse of our neighbor's and they fit everything in their midsize.

Look self, let us get serious the airline is not even playing around anymore. They are charging by weight and some fifty to a hundred dollars for additional weight. It is fine just charge it on the credit cards for now. We now begin to evaluate the weight load we are carrying around. Maybe downsizing things is not so bad, it is not like I have time. Who travels with all this weight anyways? Between career, husband, babies, grocery shopping, bills, the bills they never stop coming, diapers, bottles and sleep. Anyway, what in the world is sleep? What once carried much weight to be in the crowd or above, or even blended in the crowd now is replaced with utter exhaustion to keep up. What has gotten into you, are you not much for crowd pleasing?

At last, we have hit our forties and above. The twenties, everything financed and glamoured over are now either paid off or never made it to the payoff date. The things of the twenties were old news to the thirties, and needed to be extinguished, exchanged or upgraded. The things of the thirties are comfortable and seem to be fitting quite well in my life with a little tarnish on them. Hello, forties. Wait, I am returning home with one single suitcase? Why, is my suitcase slightly smaller yet less full?

No longer will I seek approval or opinions from the crowd. No longer will I covet what my neighbor has. No longer will I live paycheck to paycheck. No longer will I live to pay just the interest. I am certainly much more well-traveled and have traded suitcase sizes in for knowledge and wisdom. I am aware of the hidden weight fees and I am aware of the size of suitcase I will travel and return with. My focus is no longer jealousy, greed or envy. Now I desire to live within the weight regulations for luggage. What is original about the suitcase you are lugging around? God called and would like the original design He created in you back. Not the well made up, worldly accomplished versions of yourself.

FINAL WORD: I pray you understand that comparison will always make you feel either superior or inferior. We must remember that neither one serves God's purpose, Amen.

TAKE THE RISK

DAY 19

I'm writing to encourage you to fan into a flame and rekindle the fire of the spiritual gift God imparted to you when I laid my hands upon you. For God will never give you the spirit of fear, but the Holy Spirit who gives you mighty power, love, and self control.

— *2 TIMOTHY 1:6-7 TPT*

While recently journaling, I recognized how terribly intimidating it was to start this writing process. Around that same time, I had taken initiative in leading a ladies' fellowship night at church. At one event I had brought several magazines encouraging women to tear out pictures of things that caught their personal attention. What I then asked them to do was create a vision on a poster board with these many torn out pictures. These pictures would represent things that their hearts desired, areas they would like to see God move on now or even in the future. I wanted them to be encouraged. Reminding them throughout the evening that there was nothing too big for God to do for each one of them. I stretched myself further by showing them my boards from years prior and acknowledged where God had moved in my own life. If truth be told now to you reading this, I even had this book idea pinned to my vision board that night.

Not long after that fellowship night at church, I found myself being pulled away from what I know God had desired to produce through me. The harder I placed emphasis on time carved out to write, the enemy stepped up the game. My free time began to be robbed with more and more distractions. The harder the curve balls came in I suddenly realized the writing process is the exact thing I am called to do in this season of my life. It finally dawned on me one day, it was not the free time the enemy really wanted. All along the real bait was the writing process itself. Although the enemy used moments of fear, disbelief and many attempts to distract, my vision was ever so clear. The vision was made clear because the vision had been created, pinned in plain sight, spoken about, prayed about and now the enemy feared what you may someday read. Please allow these words I am about to say on this paper just permeate over you. If it matters to you, IT MATTERS TO GOD. It is time you take that risk!

FINAL WORD: I pray for you to know that God has not given to you a spirit of fear or timidity, but one of power, love and sound mind to take that risk, Amen.

YOU REFLECT A GIFT

DAY 20

As a face is reflected in water, so the heart reflects the real person.

— *PROVERBS 27:19 NLT*

On my oldest son's tenth birthday, he had decided on a dinner at Rainforest Cafe. He could hardly contain himself with the interaction of the forest as we sat to eat. During our meal, there was a young lady going around to tables making balloon animals. As I best remember, the anxious little guy could hardly eat as he kept eyes locked on her every move. The balloon creator moved around table to table drifting farther from ours. My husband and I watched as he tried to take bites missing his mouth over again, certain he thought he would miss his opportunity to make eye contact. My son finally drew her attention our way, she came to the edge of our table. She kindly asked him what it was he wanted her to make for him. He replied a "snake." My husband and I mouthed to each other a "snake."

Now this little guy has been orca whale everything since age two. The crafty young lady whipped out a balloon, a little air there and a knot here and twist there, boom the snake appeared. My son just grinned ear to ear. During the young lady's short balloon making stay at the edge of our table I was in awe of her hair. My thoughts kept repeating "wow her hair is really cool." Completely out of left field my husband spoke up and said to her, "your hair is really cool." Immediately sitting back in my chair, glancing at him then her. It was then her eyes filled with tears. She said, "thank you I have been very ill recently." She went on to share that she had been seeing doctors and her hair has continued to fall out so shaving most of it was a very recent decision. It was such a recent decision—as in yesterday recent. She explained she had been feeling very self- conscious about it throughout the day and these kind words made her day.

Next, our little family spoke up and asked her if we could just pray with her. In that moment she graciously obliged. As we checked out of the restaurant she continued to pass by tables in our direction and gently handed us her contact information. She asked if we would keep her in our prayers and we agreed to do so. The way God works is never within the routine of our table setting.

I am a hairdresser by trade so it would have been very easy for me to express a liking to her hair. Yet God did something even bigger than that. God chose to use a ten-year old to ask for a snake balloon, that clearly revealed the enemy lurking around the young ladies' confidence. God did not even choose to use eyes trained to see beauty. God chose to use the eyes of a man simply because he knew what this young lady needed to hear at that exact moment. But what God did next was use us as part of His family, to show her His glorious light. How glorious is our God! Would you invite God in to use you at your table?

FINAL WORD: I pray you allow God to have His way in all of life's celebrations big and small, Amen.

BREAKTHROUGH

DAY 21

When the woman realized she couldn't hide any longer, she came and fell trembling at Jesus' feet. Before the entire crowd she declared, "I was desperate to touch you, Jesus, for I knew if I could just touch even the fringe of your robe I would be healed." Jesus responded, "Beloved daughter, your faith in me has released your healing. You may go with my peace."

— LUKE 8:47-48 TPT

In the year 2016, I had just walked into a diagnosis called rheumatoid arthritis. Some may be familiar with this but in case not here is what it is: a chronic inflammatory disorder affecting many joints including hands and feet. The body's immune system attacks its own tissues and joints. If left uncontrolled it can attack organs too. At the time of this diagnosis, I had battled a few years of pain, causing me now to be at a place I could not even sit and cross my legs without pain.

After seeking three different doctors' opinions, they had all come to the same diagnosis. At the time I had been receiving treatment through several types of medication. Of these treatments some had been around for years to treat malaria. These medications were not even touching the pain or giving me any comfort. The next step of treatment would be offered to me through an injection. I would need to give this to myself either in the stomach or leg, once every two weeks. Coming in agreement yet again to this treatment plan and ending with very little comfort between doses.

Going back several times and explaining that I had seen little to no change, I was offered only additional medications to add to those I was already taking. After roughly a six-month period of giving it more time the next treatment the doctors came up with would be chemotherapy in pill form. I remember listening to what the doctor was trying to tell me and my mind wandered to the worst place ever. I could not help but think this cannot be. There had to be another way, and I was desperate for a breakthrough from God. I left the doctor's office that day with a list of yet more medications that I would need to start taking to boost my immune system before this first treatment.

As I drove up to the pharmacy that day I just remember crying out to God for help, saying, "I will believe you for my healing Lord, just heal me please Lord." Stepping foot out of the car and walking in the pharmacy, I shared with my pharmacist that I would not be picking up these medications today or any day. My relationship with the pharmacist was quite open since he had been handling all my prior medications. From what I knew of the pharmacist he was a kind Christian. The words replied to me struck me differently that day, "Are you sure this isn't the calm before the storm?" I remember thinking, you bet it is, because my Jesus is about to do something miraculous, watch and see.

When I arrived home, I grabbed my Bible and started digging for a word from God to hang on to. I came across this verse in Isaiah 53:5 "and by His stripes we are healed." I took liberty in creating 3x5 flashcards and placing them around my house. The cards hung everywhere, on my mirrors, nightstands, and food cupboards. No matter the level of pain that came at me, I wanted to be reminded of what God was still doing every moment of my day. Throwing out every medication that was given to me under this diagnosis and breaking covenant with it, I picked up my new diagnosis, "By His Stripes I Am Healed." A few months later I returned to my primary care doctor for routine blood. Things were significantly improving over my health. I was asked what medications I was taking? My immediate reply was NOTHING! I am pretty sure if looks alone could have stopped a freight train it would have at that moment. I had shared how I turned it over to God and by His stripes, I was healed. I was then led down the hall to do blood work. Before we departed these words were spoken over me. "We will need to check your increased levels." Instantly thinking "increased levels" absolutely not! I break that off in the name of Jesus and By His Stripes I Am Healed in Jesus Name.

Walking away from the doctor's office that day I remember knowing my story was once like the woman with the blood issue written in Scripture that day. Jesus said, "you may go with my peace." I walked away with my peace. That same week I got a call and the results given were, "no further bloodwork will be needed." Glory be to God my breakthrough had arrived! What breakthrough

might you be waiting for? Your faith in God has released your healing!

FINAL WORD: I pray that every spiritual thing you battle with be covered now by the blood of Jesus and that by His stripes you are healed, Amen.

DEEP WATERS

DAY 22

When you go through deep waters, I will be with you. When you go through rivers of difficulty, you will not drown. When you walk through the fire of oppression, you will not be burned up; the flames will not consume you.

— *ISAIAH 43:2 NLT*

There had come a season in my marriage where my husband and I had drifted into deep and murky waters. Our marriage could no longer withstand the same way we had been doing it all those years. The arguments were longer, the scars were cutting deeper, and the battles were being stretched onto the shoulders of our loved ones. One night after a long drawn out fight I had reached a place where I no longer felt I wanted or even could go on in the marriage. Removing myself to the couch for the night I remember just falling into a profuse state of weeping, this kind of weeping was like nothing I have ever experienced since. I gazed to the ceiling in the room and began crying out loud to God with these words "Lord I cannot keep doing this anymore and I cannot keep going on like this."

Suddenly, as if I was now encountering an out of body experience the scene shifted with an overwhelming amount of comfort, compassion and love washing into the room and pouring out over me. I knew that until now, I had not ever been in a place like this place felt to me. What I saw next above me in the room was the image of two hands cupped and coming my way. They were coming, wrapping me tightly and bringing comfort. The hands that I was now cupped in began to carry me and I felt as if I was not in the room any longer. I felt like I was no longer on the couch but that these gentle hands had become my couch. I knew these hands and I was floating in the comforting hands of my Father. Through a series of cloud formations, we traveled together, me resting peacefully in His hands as along the clouds we drifted, still cupped in the hands of overwhelming love. The hands of my Father were then taking me up to a bright beam of light, setting me upright in place. As I stood tall and upright in the bright light before Him, I heard words I know now spoken in my Spirit "This is as far as I can take you, I cannot take you any farther." I suddenly realized the encounter I just had experienced was the Father's love for me. I certainly have no recollection of drifting off to sleep that night, but when I woke in the morning, there I lay on the couch. One thing I was certain of there was plenty of work to be done on my part. I got on the old whistle, as some might say, and started reaching out to Christian counselors. Focused to work on me first, I began through an extensive weekly process to heal old wounds. I had the habit of allowing these old wounds to bleed over into my marriage and other areas in my life. It was not very long before my husband took notice of the change and transformation. My husband was now willing to offer his part in this healing process.

This new Christ-centered process of healing and seeking counseling left us open to a new area in our marriage. Grace, it was welcome in our marriage, in our home, with our children, in every area it was welcome to bleed over. Today we celebrate seventeen years married and twenty-two years together. We have not always gotten it all right, over, and over again. What we have gotten right is room for more Grace over again. There is a place that God will meet with you every time. We must be willing to go halfway. Remember GRACE wins every time!

FINAL WORD: I pray for your understanding, that to obtain more Grace you are choosing today to allow for all the old ways of handling things to die off, Amen.

YOU ARE STRONGER THAN YOU BELIEVE

DAY 23

Then God looked over all he had made, and he saw that it was very good! And evening passed and morning came, marking the sixth day.

— *GENESIS 1:31 NLT*

I recently came across this quote from an unknown author: "A bird sitting on a tree is never afraid of the branch breaking because her trust is not in the branch but on its own wings."[1] Always believe in yourself.

Reading this just one time is never good enough for me. I find myself referencing this quote often. For just a moment could you return to the beginning, see that in Genesis chapter one, which is the beginning, God created all things. At the end of Genesis chapter one, we are told God looked over all he made, not just some of what he made, "all of what he made." He saw that it was very good!

If I were to ask you to rate your level of belief that all of what God made is very good, what would that look like for you? Would you say yesterday it was a ten but man today it is looking a little more like a five because my car did not start. Or maybe last week it was a three because your husband got ill, and the laundry piled up and the kids were late for games. I am not sure what your weeks appear to be like or even hour by hour for that matter. What I do know is we all waver on the charts of belief. We all have the days that are tens and we all have a cluster of threes.

What I also understand is this, to have the opportunity to experience more days that are a ten I am going to have to adjust a bit. I may even need to give the old mind set a swift boost. I may even need to get the mind aligned to my heart while I am at it. The words I am declaring to happen for that day may look and sound off a little like this: "today, today, the one I'm in today, no matter the circumstances, will be a ten." Of course, the day may only actually appear to be a three. But I am not going to let the day know it is anything different than a ten. I am going to search out every bright moment in the circumstances and I will not be shaken down the number line. Each day will have the needs already met and the agenda precisely in the hands of the Creator.

My agenda, what was I even thinking, it belongs to the Lord. I will walk in belief knowing that according to God's daily planner, yes, I said God has a daily planner, for my days, and yes, He already scored them a ten. Because, if God created all things according to His word and it was good, then today and every day that was created for me and even you was designed a ten and nothing less. Remember, God looked over everything and gave it no less than one hundred percent and said it was good. Today my friend is better than good!

. . .

FINAL WORD: *I pray that you will gather up strength and belief to endure the weight upon your wings in this day, Amen.*

MADE IT

DAY 24

It takes a grinding wheel to sharpen a blade, and so one person sharpens the character of another.

— *PROVERBS 27:17 TPT*

Today I want to encourage you to look at your spouse, a parent, a family member or even any given relationship you might have walked through that involved feelings toward another. We were created for relationship. But we also have a tendency to table relationships we just might have been created for. As a daughter, wife, mother and friend I struggle from time to time within the relationship roles of all these titles. One is not better than the other and one does not hold more power than another. As a daughter, my responsibility within those perimeters evolves as I develop and mature in that role. I may be partaking in the relationship to learn the gift of honoring another, perhaps my Father and Mother, or as caregiver. As a wife, that relationship could be to learn the gift of serving, caring, team building together and accommodating one another's needs. As a mother, I am to demonstrate the gift of gentleness, comfort, compassion, kindness, wisdom, strength, correction and courage. The relationship gift of the friend may look like a source of love, compassion, communication, healing, joy and encouragement at times. The lines amongst all these can and will bleed into each other as we mature in each area.

That is the beauty behind participating in relationships. Within these various relationships, we learn something here on earth about one another. A few things that relationships here on earth can and at some point, will teach all is this. If you choose to stick around in a relationship long enough it will teach you the differences between one another, but God will teach you about similarities in others. You will learn what struggle feels like, but God will teach you what victory looks like through others. You will learn the emotion of pride amongst one another, but God will show you what humility looks like in one. You will experience what jealousy feels like and God will show you what security is like. You will experience what separation is like, yet God will show you what unity is like. You will know what anger feels like and God will show you what forgiveness looks like. Finally, you will know what loss feels like, but God will show you a home for the lost.

Now, if you have read this far then I am certain you are by now interested in the uncovering of the hidden treasure. The treasure is found within each relationship. The treasure is sometimes you may just be the grinding wheel and other times you may be the blade. In moments when life dulls your edges, you will reach back for skills taught in past relationships that forged those character edges.

. . .

FINAL WORD: I pray for every Godly relationship encounter you experience and that a little bit of them strengthens a lot more of you, Amen.

REFINED

DAY 25

If we are thrown into the blazing furnace, the God whom we serve is able to save us. He will rescue us from your power, Your Majesty. But even if he doesn't, we want to make it clear to you, Your Majesty, that we will never serve your gods or worship the gold statue you have set up."

— *DANIEL 3:17-18 NLT*

If you have not yet been tested in your arena of faith, please consider the phrase "all in due time." We are never fully capable of talking about the victory unless we have become victors. All victories are won in battle. Take for instance, our service men and women who proudly honor our country with their lives. Many return home with medals of honor for the bravery demonstrated through victorious battles protecting our freedom of— yours and mine. Some may argue the fact that these men and woman have a choice. Fair enough, but are we free of a choice too? Absolutely, we have the choice where we will serve in the end too. Will it be Heaven or Hell? It is deep in the stories of those who left the footprints before us that we read in the word, who have been tried to the utmost degree that can still come out and write about how God led them through the victory. Take the well talked about story of Shadrach, Meshach, and Abednego in the book of Daniel. They refused to serve Nebuchadnezzar's other gods and despite the refusal to worship the gold statue they were tried. Because of their disobedience to King Nebuchadnezzar, they were ordered to be thrown into the fiery furnace. Plot twist, God was in the furnace. I am not certain what trial or trials you may be up against today. I am not even certain about your tomorrows let alone my own or the trials of next year or even years from now. This I know for certain, if you choose God, in every trial you face, you will partner with good company every time. The trial process will also bring opportunity for refinement. With just the right amount of heat we all become transformed on the other side. Will you choose to endure the process or allow the process to endure you? The world longs for the beauty of a precious stone.

Final Word: I pray you feel comforted through the refinement process, Amen.

HEART OF STONE

DAY 26

I will give you a new heart and put a new spirit within you; I will take the heart of stone out of your flesh and give you a heart of flesh.

— *EZEKIEL 36:26 NKJV*

In the age of today it is so easy to have swelled heads and boastful attitudes. We are, have been, or can be boastful because of just about anything. Elevating ourselves and our accomplishments higher than God. Careers we have, the car we drive, the house we live in, the money we stash or flash, the crowds we keep, or even the leadership roles we take. Ask yourself at this pivotal moment, has something been elevated to a high place, something that is more like an idol or god? Are you now questioning everything in your life? Please beloved, do not take it that far.

Recently while studying the back half, chapters in the book of Ezekiel I ran across a story. I know I have breezed over it many times before. There was a city called Tyre. The city had a king and there were also leaders. Tyre's king particularly became linked to a chief sin. Many of us, myself included can easily relate to this sin called pride. Spiritually speaking the king just had a heart problem that led to his own path of destruction. Why did his path lead to destruction? Because he was playing on team satan and his role of influence poured out upon his beloved community.

Stop and pause a moment. I had to ask myself if I could remember a time and place in my own life where identity placement elevated higher than God. Of course, there was and if you asked me if anyone could have convinced me to change my heart otherwise, I would have fought with every tooth and nail to stay committed to my ways.

In chapter 28 The New King James Bible states in the very first four verses, countless numbers of you, yours, and yourselves. The king of Tyre developed a heart that was lifted up, because he chose to put himself as god. Through his own efforts he gained riches for himself, increased his own riches in line with his own wisdom and understanding, and his heart was lifted-up because of all the riches. For some of us and I am talking directly to myself here too, God has sent people like Ezekiel to straighten out matters of the heart. Unfortunately, in my own life I was one of the "yous" in this scenario, chasing after that participation trophy. Can you relate? The king of Tyre believed he was god. Sadly, he had to endure the consequences of elevating himself to such a high place.

When wise people get close to God, they develop a dependency on Him for ALL THINGS. When our hearts become filled with the Word of God the overflow pours out. Just the opposite happens when we are filling are heads with things that we think the heart wants. If our minds are telling our hearts to be full of careers, cars, money or fame then the overflow will be to elevate the heart in such manner to acquire such things, placing material or prideful desires above God. If you choose the Word of God over the worldly gods, this type of heart will demonstrate a love life pouring out for God and others. You will be transformed from the taker to the partaker of all good things. Spend a little alone time with God working on the matter of the heart. Great possibilities await those who are moved in the outpouring of a heart developed in The Word of God.

FINAL WORD: I pray for the hearts of stones to be transformed to flesh for all God's people, Amen.

THE LORD'S PRAYER

DAY 27

In this manner, therefore, pray:

Our Father in heaven, hallowed be Your name. Your kingdom come. Your will be done on earth as it is in heaven. Give us this day our daily bread. And forgive us our debts, as we forgive our debtors. And do not lead us into temptation, but deliver us from the evil one. For Yours is the kingdom and the power and the glory forever Amen.

— *MATTHEW 6:9-13 NKJV*

Maybe for you a similar story has a great emphasis to you. Church was not a big thing in my walk growing up. I think I could count on maybe two fingers the times that I attended church as a younger child. I grew up in a town that offered a very country-like lifestyle of living. About a mile from where I lived were slightly larger mountain ranges and below the mountain top sat an open horse arena below. Both times I can ever remember attending church was at this location for Sunrise Easter Service. I cannot say that I could relate church with much good either. On both occasions, the house erupted with fighting the morning of and it was cold, dewy and a far distance away. On both occasions, I remember thinking, "is God that cold and is He really that far away?" What I did take away though, as a young girl, is the Lord's Prayer.

Although I never attended church, I can remember from a young age the teaching of the Lord's prayer. I had no idea about prayer in general nor was I ever taught the importance of prayer. In the home I grew up in I learned to recite this prayer every single night before bedtime. Not to mention it became a great asset later in life during sporting events to participate with the crowd. Older and into my teen years I have shared earlier on my home life split. The now older version had me reaching into my younger years to grab hold of the foundation set in place from one single prayer. The Lord's prayer would not be forgotten. Frequently, in my days the Lord's prayer found a way back into my mouth when the circumstances around felt unbearable. Growing wiser to the new conditions and circumstances playing out around me and perhaps maturity having a part, I began to take notice that in saying this prayer there was a subtle shift of peace.

As time passed, I began to take into consideration that the Father in Heaven was not that far away, nor was He cold. Not because I could tell you where the Lord's prayer was located or that it was from the Bible, or who I was saying it to. It was all because the way the Lord's prayer made me feel when I would say it over again. Can you remember your first encounter with the Lord's prayer or a Scripture you were taught? I challenge you that if you do not know the Lord's prayer turn in your Bible or google Matthew 6:9-13. Jesus gave this prayer to His disciples instructing them if they did not know how to pray then pray this way. You're off to a great start!

FINAL WORD: I pray whatever the need is, it shall be established as it is in Heaven, Amen.

GOD STILL MOVES

DAY 28

But let patience have its perfect work, that you may be perfect and complete, lacking nothing.

— *JAMES 1:4 NKJV*

Many things throughout life we cannot even begin to predict nor understand the movements around us. In fact, this very moment that you are reading this entry today many life altering circumstances may be taking place in your own life or in a loved one's. May I lend my heartfelt compassion to you in this moment and say whatever is happening at this very moment that feels worse than good I am sorry. Please know that if I could reach through these pages and pull you in for a hug and say it will all be okay I would. These unprecedented situations leave us feeling that life can be less than perfect. You may be searching for some sort of clarity over a matter or even praying for God to show you a glimpse of hope at this given moment. Let me assure you that you are not the only one recruiting a search team. Allow me to say this "be patient." Patience is a virtue and to develop that virtue you must endure the process along the way to get there. When it is not clear that our needs, our prayers or our petitions are being heard or met on our time frame how does patience work into that?

Patience is not the first response for me either. It is usually the last-ditch effort after all my other efforts failed. The truest definition of patience is God. The dictionary defines patience as "the capacity to accept or tolerate delay, trouble, or suffering without getting angry or upset."[1] Refer back to the true definition of patience, it is God. Why might I choose God for this definition? Answer: because when I did not choose Him all the times before, He chose me. When I could not tolerate one more positive thing said about God, He tolerated my rejection with patience. When I chose sin over Him, God tolerated my choices with patience. When my choices were to run far, wide and forever long from the One who suffered it all for me, He waited it out with patience. Patience alone in our own measure of strength cannot and will not ever work. Allowing God to work patience in and along our journey through constant prayer and communication with Him works on time all the time. You are now ready for your encounter with patience. Allow patience to do a perfect work in your life leaving you lacking nothing, built from the foundation called in the waiting.

FINAL WORD: I pray for you to meet the gift of patience setting you forth in completion lacking nothing, Amen.

RE-ROUTING

DAY 29

Finally, brethren, whatever things are true, whatever things are noble,
whatever things are just, whatever things are pure, whatever things are
lovely, whatever things are of good report, if there is any virtue and if
there is anything praiseworthy-meditate on these things.

— *PHILIPPIANS 4:8 NKJV*

For some of you, the ocean is not something you may even consider setting your sight on, let alone visiting. Each year I get a great big belly laugh from my husband because he is absolutely one of those who has no desire for the ocean or the beach. Growing up in southern California, the beach was just another part of life. Times were well spent in the sun, sand and water. Looking back now, there was always something so beautiful about the beach to me. From the smell in the air, to the sound of the crashing waves. To the call of the seagulls, to the warm sun at your back. To the boards in the surf, the ships in the distance, and the laughter of children echoing at play covered in the itty-bitty grains of sand.

When the distance of the shoreline expands to the open sea it is more than the eye can fathom. I always found great joy in watching and counting the boats disappearing into the haze above the sea. There was something so majestic and beautiful as they sailed on and on. Take a glance into a recent or even current situation and picture a large boat at sea. With such a vast endless body of water and such power, the sea and the waves possess all year round, why does the boat stay afloat and not sink? If you answered because the water must have an access point inside, you are on the mark. The world and the situations we come up against are a lot like this analogy too. If you do not allow to choose the negativity to enter your vessel my friend, you will continue to sail on and on. Stay focused on whatever is true, noble, just, pure, lovely and of good report. Anything not worthy of praise must be sent out to sea to get re-routed.

Final Word: I pray for your vessel to stay afloat in all forecasted weather conditions, Amen.

PAIRED

DAY 30

Before I was humbled I used to always wander astray, but now I see the wisdom of your words. Everything you do is beautiful, flowing from your goodness; teach me the power of your wonderful words!

— PSALM 119:67-68 TPT

As I sit here writing today's devotional, I am extremely humbled in the works of God. Completely un-intentionally planned for day thirty to have such correlation, but I know again first-hand God did it! It has been a few years ago that I had been given a beautiful prayer journal from a dear friend. I absolutely loved what this journal stood for and quickly found myself ordering more like it as gifts.

The one I was most drawn to was the thirty-day prayer journal for husbands. I purchased and received it and immediately began my recordings. Each day I would record a written prayer over my husband and continued the pattern in the journal and over the next thirty days. The idea at the end of the thirty days would be to surprise him with it. As clear as yesterday I remember the thirtieth day fell on May 20th and that also happened to be his birthday. As I handed over this recorded prayer journal personalized for him, we stood that morning in our front yard overlooking our large stock tank on the property. What appeared on that tank next was like nothing we had ever witnessed, thirty Canadian geese were floating peacefully in the waters.

What a beautiful God encountered moment we were witnessing before us as a pair. God showing up and showing off, like only He can do shifted our emotions to great honor and praise. The recorded thirty-day prayers were to honor my husband and shower him with prayers of protection and a devotion of love for who he is to me. God heard all my conversations for thirty days prior. God saw them all thirty days prior and had His voice heard in all thirty days prior. It was on the thirtieth day God wanted to reveal Himself to us in all His Glory. All Glory be to God forever and ever Amen! What is it that God just may be wanting to show you in the natural, because of your obedience to Him in private?

FINAL WORD: I pray for your eyes to experience all the ways the Lord loves you and moves on your prayer behalf, Amen.

BETTER TOGETHER

DAY 31

I appeal to you, brothers and sisters, in the name of our Lord Jesus Christ, that all of you agree with one another in what you say and that there be no divisions among you, but that you be perfectly united in mind and thought.

— *1 CORINTHIANS 1:10 NIV*

Have you wondered if the main instigator of fear, satan himself, gets scared? The answer is YES! And the smell of unity attracts him. You know what is even scarier to satan than that? A united family, husband, wife, and children. This is satan's worst nightmare. Why? Because he no longer has any gain for grounds of division. There is a greater force of power, movement, and favor when you and your family come into complete unity.

A few years back my husband, children, and I were invited to a small gathering and dinner. We were the guests, and they had another set of friends coming for the evening to share a word with all of us attending. Upon arriving we were invited to sit and share in a meal, dessert, and fellowship. After the meal we were invited to gather in the living room area for a little worship and the Lord's word. Not long into worship one gentleman that played guitar asked if he could share a word with us over our family. We immediately agreed to the offer. The shared message was when our family first walked in that evening, he immediately discerned an anointing dripping from us. Going on to share that the anointing was so heavy on our family it could choke a moose to death. We were quite taken aback with the statement used and several even chuckled (including us) at the analogy but we understood it clearly. What this statement spoke was what now I believe to be complete truth. Unity releases an attractive aroma. Have you ever felt drawn to someone because of their intimate relationship with God? There, it is that aroma that is put off that is attractive to you. If one is so unified in Christ it looks good and puts off the demeanor of good. If you want to make satan quake, become unified so, "when you or your family walks in the room together you change the atmosphere." Oh, the mighty power possessed when we walk in unity. All Glory be to God!

What power, movement, favor, and authority we carry over satan when we walk in complete unity together in Christ Jesus. Satan's bullseye is to cause division, just look at the wedge he created in Adam and Eve. Affirmation of victory in our marriage and our family was a God sent blessing to say the least, but key to moving forward is in keeping the unity. Is there something causing division within your four walls? Go ahead and issue the warrant putting that guy back behind bars and under your feet where he belongs.

. . .

FINAL WORD: I pray for a spirit of unity to overwhelm every single area of your marriages, children, family, friends, careers, and churches, Amen.

TRANSFORMATION

DAY 32

This means that anyone who belongs to Christ has become a new person.
The old life is gone; a new life has begun!

— *2 CORINTHIANS 5:17 NLT*

Webster's defines to transform as: to change the outward form or appearance; to change in character or condition or to convert.[1] When I recently studied this verse in 2 Corinthians, I asked God to display His art of transformation for me to see in the natural world. Any of you ever ask to see something and God just clocks right in? That is what I had witness to. God sent me the message in the natural by using His creation the butterfly. There are a few different transformation techniques that transpire in order to reach the fullness of the butterfly. Let us talk now about this in great length.

A butterfly must transform four times through a process before reaching its full potential. First is the egg; the butterfly must lay the egg on a leaf. The butterfly will not pick just any leaf because this will be the nutrients in the many days to come. Second, is the hatching process or larva stage. The life inside the egg is not truly a butterfly, it is a very tiny caterpillar. The caterpillar is hatched and will become reliant upon the leaf as its only source of food, growing rapidly. Third, reaching max size and stopping the eating process the caterpillar will transform into what is called a pupa or chrysalis. What appears as a shell for hibernation is true transformation taking place within. This is where the butterfly obtains its true identity. Fourth, when the pupa has fully transformed to a butterfly within the chrysalis, it now emerges revealing its true radiating identity and beauty. WOW! Praise God for such detail!

There is a process for the Jesus Christ believers to undergo as well. Is it the same sort of transformation? Somewhat. We enter a world full of sin. Once this world has had a hefty go at us, we too become a part of sin in the world. Figuratively speaking, we fight our way through the decomposed sin around us. Once we have become so enlarged and weighted down, meeting max capacity with sin, we turn to our Savior. Accepting Christ envelops us in His chrysalis. In the chrysalis, God can put our pieces beautifully back together. Once healed and transformed, God releases us into His identity to testify to the Kingdom. Which process can you best identify with? Are you ready for the transformation process?

FINAL WORD: I pray transformation to take part in your life allowing Christ's image to come forth, Amen.

SOLITUDE

DAY 33

Before daybreak the next morning, Jesus got up and went out to an isolated place to pray.

— *MARK 1:35 NLT*

The Bible does not give us an accurate number of how often Jesus was led into complete solitude to commune with His Father and pray. Certainly, in the book of Mark we read where He did though. You may be asking about the importance of this. These are reflections to our decision, making skills. Our emotional responses, our demands in careers, ministry, purchases, and just about every area of life, factor in how we care for ourselves through decision making.

When Jesus went away to be alone with the Father, He stepped into solitude and silence from all. It was an opportunity to draw ever so near to His Father. It was in this place He refueled and gathered His instructions for the days ahead. It was a place of deeper relationship and a feeling of true intimacy. What answers are you longing to know? What might solitude look like in your life? Do you invest in time of solitude? If you do not, what might your place of solitude look like? There is no right or wrong answer to any of these questions or even what it should look like. The only right answer is to give yourself permission to dream and believe for that time and place of solitude with the Father. We all need a place where we can get alone with God. We all need a timeout where we can sit with God and ask the hard questions. We all need a place where we can quiet ourselves to listen for what God might want to say. Take all the time you need but will you accept my invitation to learn to get alone with God? Start small by clocking yourself out for small increments in total quiet solitude. God has already slotted a time space out just waiting for you.

FINAL WORD: I pray that you seek and find that solitude in the ABBA Father, Amen.

THE BEST IS YET TO COME

DAY 34

That is what the Scriptures mean when they say, "No eye has seen, no ear has heard, and no mind has imagined what God has prepared for those who love him."

— *1 CORINTHIANS 2:9 NLT*

Struggles with finances, struggles in my career, struggles with my family, struggles mothering my children, and even real struggles within my marriage. Every day, life is a struggle and if someone had told me the best is yet to come, I would have completely disagreed. Financially overwhelmed, consumed with debt and living check to check. In the early stages of building my career, I had minimal amounts of work. Rent felt due every time I turned around. Not to mention the cries from all my family's needs. The children, the unhappy cries of daycare to home and home to daycare. Wait, my marriage, how did it fall to shambles?

I just described my early years of finances, career, family, children and marriage. Can you relate? I would have given up a whole lot earlier had something not taken place first. In place of my finances, career, family, children and marriage was God. God had a place, and it was first place. A steady voice in the desolate times I was in, God was my knight in shining armor, telling me my best is yet to come.

Your best is yet to come. Invite God in the place of the things that take up all that wasted space. Marriage, children, family, career, and finances will always fight for first place. God will not compete nor fight with these things. He will have the final say over all things. Offer God your best, allowing Him in the place of all things and remember He will have to be nothing less than first place.

> There are no draws with God, no split decisions. When we wrestle with the Almighty, we lose. He is the undefeated champion of the universe.[1]
>
> — *R.C. SPROUL*

Final Word: I pray that your best is yet to come and that you have a get up and not a give up, Amen.

SIT UNDER MY TEACHING

DAY 35

As Jesus and the disciples continued on their way to Jerusalem, they came to a certain village where a woman named Martha welcomed him into her home. Her sister, Mary, sat at the Lord's feet, listening to what he taught.

— *LUKE 10:38-39 NLT*

Before moving my personal business next door to my home, I heard the Lord's words clearly while sitting in my time of solitude with Him. God said, "I will elevate you to a new platform." Those words in that moment reflected vivid clarity. Though, it had not been clear yet, God was getting ready to do something spectacular. I had shared many months prior with some in my circle of a strong desire to move my work to my home. Much excitement and encouragement poured in from the voices surrounding me which led my confidence to shift. After weeks of prepping myself for this big move I was beginning the work of construction that would be needed to create a new space. One evening, after a long day's work, a process of restoration was taking priority outside under the open sky. Painting old barn wood was no hard form of art, but after about two hundred painted white boards the sky looked much more appealing than the rustic slivers of wood.

Have you ever looked up to the sky and admired the cloud formations taking place above? Catching my eye, the one and only visible cloud in the sky that evening painted an art masterpiece. Pausing in the middle of my paintbrush strokes and shifting all my attention to this one individual cloud. I watched the cloud form the face of an angelic being. The cloud took on formation of hands, then face and lips until every visible detail fell into shape. As the cloud danced along in the evening sky, I caught but another word from the Lord, instructing to "sit under His teaching." Reflecting to the word previously shared with me during my quiet time with the Lord about a new platform, the bigger picture had finally puzzle pieced formation. Coming into a new location, standing on a new platform while still doing my same line of work, I would need some new level teaching and guidance along this journey. God encounters are meant to be seen. God is not trying to hide anything from you. In fact, God is asking you to search a little for what it is He wants to personally say to you. The real challenge is the way we get into posture to see Him. This is only by looking up child of God!!!

FINAL WORD: I pray you look up child of God, Amen.

PRAYERS GO UP & BLESSINGS
COME DOWN

DAY 36

*Now all glory to God, who is able, through his mighty power at work
within us, to accomplish infinitely more than we might ask or think.
Glory to him in the church and in Christ Jesus through all generations
forever and ever! Amen.*

— *EPHESIANS 3:20-21 NLT*

Have you ever sat in observation of the world
around you? I remember as a child who grew up
in Southern California the experiences from
the shopping malls. Every school year I would experience my yearly trip to the mall to get my flashy school
attire. The noises that echoed throughout the entire
building could be so distracting. Then there was always
the food court where, well forget it you would have been
better off signing to your neighbor for conversation.
Much too much noise involved with every voice striving
to be heard. Push mute and read this, you will never have
to fight to have a word with God. All lines of communication are always available twenty-four hours a day, seven
days a week, three hundred sixty-five days a year. Do you

fear the overage charges? What about the dropped calls? Then what is keeping you on hold?

Prayers have a direct line of communication straight to God and are always in network. Invested prayers for personal needs hit the emergency line. Protection, your marriage, your children, family members, extended family members, your community, your leaders, your churches, or even your children's children, all have direct access to God's telephone line with no call waiting. What then is keeping you on hold so long?

Based on this Scripture verse our most effective use of prayers sent up reflect the greatest influence on events still to come. Do not take the bait that God is not at work or able to work on things all at the same time for all His people. God is the multitasker of the now and of all things still in the future. Prayers you invest in today will manifest and accomplish infinitely more in generations yet to come. Pray for your spouse or for the one, not yet here, pray for your children, or the ones not yet here, pray about all things, so God can accomplish in your life what is promised to you, and even more then we might ask for or think for generations to come. There is plenty of room on the line! Make use of the toll-free line to God!

FINAL WORD: I pray you pick up the line and make the call, Amen.

NOT FINISHED

DAY 37

*Still, God, you are our Father. We're the clay and you're our potter. All of
us are what you made us.*

— ISAIAH 64:8 MSG

At our end, God meets us with His beginning. I
am asking some of you today a tough question.
Did you meet God at your end? Do you
remember the appearance, the sound, the taste or
perhaps the feel? Your end, was it a home you could no
longer afford, a car you could no longer pay for, a debt
you could not settle, a check that bounced, bare
cupboards, career loss, medical bills, health problems, a
loss of a father, mother, spouse or child? Was your end in
that divorce or something so unbearable it is never to
have a voice to ever again?

I take great honor for God showing me my gift early on in
my career path. It is with a posture of humility that I am
awarded the opportunity to stand behind so many while I
work. The stories that are told of love, loss and heartache

have helped me develop a strategic plan in prayer for the countless stories woven into my days and weeks. Although I do not remember every face, story, or tear that has fallen, I never forget the sounds, the tastes and the feel of every story told. Though the clients in my seat may change, their personal stories mimic the next and the next. They all have a similar appearance, a familiar sound, a bitter taste and aching pain to them. The stories have been commonly threaded by the power of darkness by the enemy who comes to steal, kill and destroy hope within the people of God. Having all the right answers is not my job but it is my job to remind others that God is good always. Please, beloved child of God, if it is not beautiful, then God is not finished. He is the Creator of all beautiful things. Pick yourself up and get yourself back on the potter's wheel, and allow the potter to complete the work of clay in His hand.

FINAL WORD: I pray you allow the potter time at the wheel to form the clay, Amen.

PRESS ON

DAY 38

You have stayed with me in my time of trial.

— *LUKE 22:28 NLT*

Which one, which time and when will it ever end? Famous last words right up until the very next trial threatens to hit. Have you been told you can possess great power in trials? Yes friend, I have been told this too. These words fly off the tongue so freely when the one sharing them is walking on the other side of their trial and rejoicing in freedom.

Just think about the year 2020 for instance. We all remember it well, a pandemic the world some experts say had never been seen before. Now I am not certain I fully believe that statement. We all possibly have grandparents, great grandparents, and great-great grandparents, that experienced certain pandemics in their times too. I recently read an article about The Flu Pandemic of 1918-1919. It was during World War 1 and called "Spanish flu", suggesting it had started in Spain. Three to five percent of the world's population died, around 17 million deaths due to this virus.

As a nation in 2020, to state it with simplicity, it seemed like we were all put on temporary house arrest, causing lost jobs, household incomes drained, everyday supplies limited, deaths occurring to loved ones, children were out of school for months and parents took on the role of teachers. Not to mention the health scare, mask frenzy that swept through households dividing families from gathering the way they traditionally had.

Summed up by our churches vacated and leaders targeted, little more than one trial we might just say. More along the lines of a state of emergency would you agree? Before, you a laundry list just aired, falling into a category five catastrophic trial if I ever lived through one. But let us acknowledge again the stories once told of these kinds of things. If the ones who shared these stories had not lived through them, then what story would be left to tell? God uses them all. While you close the book on today, read on a little further with me, hear not me, but what God wants to say to you. I stayed with you in your time of trial. Because you are reading the words on this page is proof enough that God still stayed!

FINAL WORD: I pray you are no longer hostage to the trials, Amen.

LET'S GO DOWN TO THE WATER

DAY 39

With joy you will drink deeply from the fountain of salvation!

— *ISAIAH 12:3 NLT*

The year 2011 was a magnificent year. It was the year that I took in a drink and felt the quenching of thirst like ever before. I share with you an encounter that forever changed my life. This experience was like nothing I had experienced before or likely will never again. The week of August 7th had not felt much different than the rest because I was cleaning house. The difference was what took place during cleaning. While vacuuming, I felt something quite unusual come over me. An overwhelmingly intense emotion to get myself clean and clean now! Trying to shake the sudden urgency, I proceeded vacuuming. No longer able to ignore the urge I felt, I grabbed a broom and went to the porch. Flooding emotions swept over me reducing me to a puddle of tears.

Returning to the house, immediately I called the neighbor on the phone, but no answer. Still shaken and overwhelmed with emotion, I dialed a friend. Unclear how to proceed, I placed a phone call to my pastor. I chuckle a bit now as I share this with you. I shared all my symptoms with my kind pastor as he patiently listened through the snot and sobbing. What I had shared and what he could understand led him to understand that I was ready to drink from the fountain of salvation. Sunday, August 7, 2011 I chose to go down to the river and receive the greatest gift of Salvation.

Maybe you have had a similar encounter or maybe you are in search of just a touch or encounter with God. Either way I say this to you, "Won't you drink with me from the fountain of salvation?" I long for you to hear the words "Welcome home beloved child of God."

FINAL WORD: I pray you say these words aloud if you have not yet received Christ into your heart and your life. Father, I am a sinner in need of your forgiveness. I believe that you came to earth as a man and rose up on the third day conquering death. I accept you in my heart and to be a part of my life. I ask for your forgiveness and to be forgiven of all my sins. I repent and turn away from sinning and all my wrong doings. Jesus, I ask you to come into my heart and into my home and be my Lord and Savior! Fill me with the Holy Spirit. I thank you Lord that I am now sealed in the blood of Jesus, Amen.

STILL TRUST

DAY 40

Jesus said to him, "Away from me, Satan! For it is written: 'Worship the Lord your God, and serve him only.'"

— *MATTHEW 4:10 NIV*

H ave you ever been robbed? What happen to your ability to trust? Several times over the course of your life you will feel as if you have been robbed. If I was a betting woman, and I am not, but right about now you are revisiting the old robbery files, aren't you? Well stop it! The list will continue to drag you down and out. We view robbery like we did not get the promotion, or the car, or the partner, or the award because they did instead, it does not matter. The list of scenarios or the final why not. The "I deserved" does not sting any less. The cycle we play over and over again is the one we simply lost out on, now we feel robbed, and the result is we give up trust.

So, what is your ammo for the plot twist? How about motivation to still trust? There is a cunning way the enemy allows you to think you have been robbed so you just might lose trust in God. Reality and truth be told, you have been spared for so much better. Guaranteed is the outcome of something received through certainty. The only thing in life that has a guarantee on it and allows us to receive anything of certainty from it is the written Word of God.

Take the plot and twist the outcome with "away from me satan." It worked for Jesus! Why in the world would you think it would not work for you? Look at Jesus who was God in the flesh and without exemption from the feel of robbery. In fact, if you will recall the scene of the forty days in the wilderness you will see satan is full of lies. He did all he could do to take the seed of trust from Jesus. Satan told Jesus if you are the Son of God, tell the stones to become bread. He took Jesus to the Holy City and said throw yourself down. Then, he took Jesus to a very high mountain peak of splendor and begged Jesus to worship him. Jesus picked up His trust and spoke "Away from me, satan! For it is written: 'Worship the Lord your God, and serve him only.'" There is your plot twist. "For it is written!" Use it beloved!

FINAL WORD: I pray your plot twist be that "it is written" against the enemy's offenses, Amen.

YOU WILL BE FAITHFUL TO PLANT
THE SEED

DAY 41

The Lord isn't really being slow about his promise, as some people think.
No, he is being patient for your sake. He does not want anyone to be
destroyed, but wants everyone to repent.

— *2 PETER 3:9 NLT*

Pre-salvation let me just say I would have judged anyone who ever tried to point me in the direction of Christ. I had a few brief childhood encounters and throughout my high school years perhaps a few more. From close girlfriends inviting me to church, I would often find any avenue with the old familiar resistant pushback of invitations right back to sin. The few times I went along to church I even participated in youth activities. My commitment level was that I showed up period. Within minutes of departing the parking lot I reverted right back to my sinful ways. Looking back now, clearly that was the devil's invitation back to his playground. Nonetheless the seeds were sown.

When my husband left the Marine Corps and shortly after we first wed, we moved to Texas. We had a close service friend that had a bit of positive influence in our relocation. During the first four-months in Texas we had all lived together. Sundays in the home were left to just husband and me. The friend spent most Sundays away fellowshipping in church and with family. As we lounged around the house during our short stay much curiosity was aroused. Another faithful seed planted.

Purchasing our own home and working in our careers we were confronted yet again. A previous co-worker of my husband's needed work. With that came another need, a place to live. Offering up a room in our home was the least we could do in return. Each day we would watch as our new roommate entered our home, escaping to a tiny corner to read The Word of God. Sundays once again were just my husband and me. There God was again, faithfully planting the seed. Are you seeing the pattern?

Yet again, just as quickly as that roommate moved out another was in. This roommate and this time would be different. This situation felt a little closer to home. There was a great sound of loss and healing taking place in our home. In the tiny little corner of our home, yet another roommate consecrated to the Lord week after week. In our home we witnessed God take what was lost and use it for His good because of this roommate's faithfulness. Again Sunday came, and we were alone. Just like before, a seed was planted.

My hope for sharing this truth is that you look back and maybe catch a small glimpse in your own story where our Lord and Savior may have been all along. Right in the comfort of our own home, my husband and I were too distant to invite Him in. God was gently still in and around every corner of the home. Can you recall the seeds along your path? God is there and in your corner.

FINAL WORD: I pray that you can trace the steps of seeds on your path, Amen.

LONG SUFFERING

DAY 42

But you belong to God, my dear children. You have already won a victory over those people, because the Spirit who lives in you is greater than the spirit who lives in the world.

— *1 JOHN 4:4 NLT*

There is probably no better time than such a time as this to share some parts of a season with you about long-suffering. Without picking apart every little detail, let us just hit some high points today. For a large portion of time, I lived in my own prison of guilt. Why? Because I was guilty by association. Throughout life I made covenant with this world. People, places and even things became my relationship focus. People in my life had complete influence on how to raise my family, run my household and even possess things. Places had been allowed to pay a visit and put a wedge in my marriage, even taking it on many places around the world. Then there were things, material things. They were welcomed to have their way in me and with me and for me, creating idolatry. In fact, I trusted the opinions alone of the people, places and things all in my life. Building my life upon the unhealthy high places of the world. Where was Jesus? Jesus who?

These matters belonged solely to the people in my life, the places they would take me, and the things that made me feel valued. As time carried on, God had something to say about all of this. That is when the greatest quake would happen in my life. That is when like the walls of Jericho, everything came crashing down around me. You might have picked up something about me in the days of reading ahead, I was not always a great listener. I really had a bad taste for finding things out the hard way, but I really enjoyed my life, my way, for way to long. For a few excruciating long years, I would sit in a period of long-suffering as the relationships were slowly detached from me. The places I once visited were forbidden to trespass. The things I desired to hold were ripped from my grip. God would show me spite of my troubles a new way.

My people would now be His people for me. The places would now be the places He prepared for me. The things would now be all the things He desired for me to have. Great loses stood in the balance but because of long-suffering, I had been given a life of balance. The most precious things we let go of have the greatest return on our relationship with God.

FINAL WORD: I pray for a return on the long-suffering you endure, Amen.

ASK

DAY 43

Ask and it will be given to you; seek and you will find; knock and the door will be opened to you.

— *MATTHEW 7:7 NIV*

I am clearly not a movie buff but when I happen to catch a great Christian based film, I try to take something out of it and see where it can be applied. Today I want to share the film *War Room* with you that I recently watched, starring the beautiful Priscilla Shirer. This film all the way through had me wanting to pause and get my own self armored up for action. Within the film I learned of a small room with four walls in the home consecrated out to do spiritual warfare. Wanting to pause the film and head for the closet to throw out everything had me a bit inspired I must say. But I waited and went somewhere else with it.

I shared with you that I had the great privilege to move my business home and that my family and I built a large portion of what is now my small shop with our own hands. When I was creating a vision for how this shop would be consecrated to and for the Lord's work, I envisioned a place to war and battle just like I had seen in this film. The space would feel warm, the space would be bright, the space would be quiet, and the space would separate itself from everything else that happened in that place. It would paint a picture of the victories won. Let me remind you that I work in an industry where I get to create beauty from ashes. So, this war room was a bonus room for me. With weeks of work and quiet times of prayer I got to escape to a place every day taking the prayers and needs of many to battle. In this room I built biblical principles around a specific verse that I would follow with each petition. I would ask the Lord for the need I was bringing before Him. I would seek after Him for it, and each time I knocked I waited for the door to be opened.

Each time I crossed the threshold of this room I met with the same verse principles painted on the wall before me. The same three principles apply in everyone's needs, whether a believer or not. We all have needs and we all come to a point to ask someone to help us fill the need. Next we must seek the thing we are initially after in order to find it, right? Lastly, when what we seek is finally found it is like the doors have swung wide open for us to make our way.

Matthew 7:7 gives us the strategic plan for victory over our battles. Let the weight of your war room be carried to "The Throne Room of God." Quoted by Rabindranath Tagore: "The one who plants trees, knowing that he will never sit in the shade, has at least started to understand the meaning of life."[1] Do not stop asking, seeking or knocking just because you have not witnessed any shade lately. It is coming. Believe for it!

FINAL WORD: I pray that you have encounters with the One who seeks to have every encounter with you, Amen.

TIME

DAY 44

There is a time for everything, and a season for every activity under the heavens.

— *ECCLESIASTES 3:1 NIV*

Timing is everything, but so is practice. If only I had a dollar for every single time I heard those words. Timing really is everything when we are moving in the realm of God's timing. In Scripture, there are several incidents that pertain to the appropriate timing of God and the results to the final outcome over a matter of time. Our entire lives are driven by the concept that it must be time. But is it the time you are saying it is or is it in the timeline of God? Do you want in on a little secret God carries? To get in time with God you must first explore God, and to explore God's timing, you first must meet up with God on His time. Basically, God makes time for all of us around the clock. When we find ourselves not at peace with what might be happening in life then whose timing are we not at peace with? Our own timing. Doubting God and thinking He may have bad timing on something is never the best use of His time. It is the best use of ours! Are you following me? The one who lives in disbelief or resentfulness over things happening out of the realm of God time is essentially living in their own time zone. The only outcome left for God is the outcome we forced ourselves into out of impatience. Since it did not happen when we thought it should have happened then we must make it happen for ourselves. Again and again, we behave according to the same pattern and wonder why the outcome is not any different. Getting into this pattern will only lead down the path of getting ahead of God and depletion of all hope and strength. Process the time of your seasons with God and pursue through with God, not doing all the maneuvering for God. If the stopwatch is always in our hand, just keep in mind that God finishes in His time, every time. All things God has for you are absolutely in perfect timing! Wait for it!

FINAL WORD: *I pray God's perfect timed moments over every season, Amen.*

YOUR WORD IS SETTLED IN HEAVEN

DAY 45

Your eternal word, O LORD, stands firm in heaven.

— *PSALM 119:89 NLT*

Severe headaches! Anyone get them? Headaches on Monday, headaches on Tuesday, headaches on Wednesday. Headaches tormented me like a bad heartbreak. From my earliest childhood memories, I remember the indentions of the little round pills that lined my pockets. Classmates would ask me to come jump rope or climb on the bars or play a loud game of handball and I would withdraw. Once married and living in Texas my husband encouraged me to go see a specialist.

Travelling to Dallas I would undergo a series of tests—bloodwork, CAT scans, MRIs and more. The results were inconclusive. Although the results led us down dead end paths, the specialist agreed to less detrimental medications. Living most of my twenties and thirties on medication I had a feeling rise up within me to approach the problem in new ways. A few years ago, I felt the Lord nudging me to believe Him for my healing. One evening before bed and taking my medications I tuned into a live Christian broadcast. The sermon was touching on healing for different illnesses.

It was toward the very end of the broadcast, a healing word was being released for those who struggled with any form of chronic headaches or migraines. Coincidence? Nope! God's perfectly timed confirmation without a doubt. Just as the words left the mouth of the speaker and made way through the airwaves, I deposited them in my spirit just like I was making a large deposit into my bank account. There is not any art to receiving your healing. It falls right in line with faith. God always sends the Holy Spirit to nudge you, just letting you in on a secret He wants to do for you. Next it is like that idea or thought you had was being confirmed again or coming back around to say hello or remember me for the second time. Last, because it was already settled with God in Heaven, you just pick it up and deposit it in your spirit just like depositing money into a bank account. When putting something into an account it is handed over and believed by faith that it was deposited, right?

Claiming my healing and disposing of all medication that night was no hard task. It had been settled and God said so. The following morning the enemy did not really like what God said. The vengeance was brutal. To this day, there never will be another debilitating pain like the one brought on the morning after claiming God's victory over my health. Although the enemy wanted my healing and the intensity of the migraine was like nothing I had felt before, I walked it, I talked it out with God, and held on to the healing the Lord promised for me. The deposit was made in my account and I was not returning my healing In Jesus Name. Heaven has your healing. You can bank on it!

FINAL WORD: I pray for you to meet with God for your healing, Amen.

NOTHING BEAUTIFUL ASKS FOR ATTENTION

DAY 46

To bring Queen Vashti to him with the royal crown on her head. He wanted the nobles and all the other men to gaze on her beauty, for she was a very beautiful woman.

— ESTHER 1:11 NLT

Let us begin today's journey in the book of Esther. There was a king by the name of Xerxes who reigned over 127 provinces from India to Ethiopia. This king ruled from his royal throne in Susa. During the third year of his reign, he had decided to throw a royal banquet for the nobles that lasted for 180 days. Immediately after the 180 days he decided to throw one for his people from the greatest to the least, lasting seven days. Picture this for a moment. It was said that all this took place in the courtyard that was beautifully decorated. Unlimited drinks were served in gold goblets with an abundance of wine, reflecting the king's generosity. At this very time the king's wife Queen Vashti gave a banquet for the women in the royal palace of King Xerxes.

Scripture tells us on the seventh day of the feast, the king was in high spirits because of the wine. We could only assume meaning drunk by this point, right? The king called for his seven eunuchs to bring Queen Vashti to him with her royal crown on her head. King Xerxes wanted to show off to the nobles and all other men and allow them to gaze at her beauty, for she was a beautiful woman. When the king's men gave her this order, she refused causing the king to burn all over in complete anger. Because of her stand some of the king's wise counsel panicked. Could it be that many women would be encouraged to follow her lead? These men suggested a decree be written to ban Queen Vashti from King Xerxes' presence and he was to have his choice of a new queen more worthy. After a sobering moment King Xerxes thought about the decree and Vashti and still chose to dismiss Queen Vashti. Some other personal staff to the king suggested they would find him a new beautiful young virgin and the king obliged. This is where the young beautiful Esther came in.

My goodness, what a bad day to be a beauty queen, literally! Every time I reread this chapter in Esther about the beautiful Queen Vashti, I really cannot even fathom what courage she must have had. I try to picture her standing there among seven serving men. I have even tried to put myself in her shoes a time or two. Not just one man, my friends, seven of the king's finest men. She was not just saying "No" to one man she was saying "No" times seven. Even though it is not stated in Scripture, this queen was not only willing to stand up for morals in a time where women had no place setting them, Queen Vashti was willing to surrender a seat in royalty for women's rights to have a voice.

Power and wealth will not lead to authority. Anything forcing one into obedience is not founded on morals. Standing up for the voiceless may cost you a seat at the table. Jesus never forced His hand of obedience upon any. Morals are on display to the world around us. What seat will you have?

FINAL WORD: I pray that all approaches made on your behalf be an act of your own free will, Amen.

KEEP GOING

DAY 47

Get all the advice and instruction you can, so you will be wise the rest of your life.

— *PROVERBS 19:20 NLT*

Are you inspired by people who pretend to not ever see you? Has being seen in the crowd been a real struggle? Personal confession, this was a hang up for me too. Popularity was not this girl, but this girl craved popularity. Surrounded by too many guy friends and little to no girlfriends. Having two brothers I just thought this was the norm for all family dynamics. Sister grows up with all brothers so sister just falls into the "Hey Bro" category.

During my teenage years, I began to realize I was encircled by a much smaller crowd than I preferred. If you were interested in the fixer upper friend, I was your girl, probably best known for making your life feel a little worse. Girls were mean, gossipy, confrontational, jealous, judgmental and ever so needy. The true friendships I did establish meant something. Those few friendships I had went deeper because I hated drama. In my home, there had been enough drama without help from any outsiders. My brothers and most of their own friends I claimed as my crew too. Maybe because I was the middle child, it was much easier to do what they did.

My brothers had friendships that looked so easy. They all were really a little rough around the edges and just told each other how it was. This type of love language did not translate to girls my age very well. Especially if you were planning for them to stay friends with you long. I can hear someone reading this now and saying, "that's me!" She gets it. Yes beloved, I absolutely get it!

The male and female sex could not be more different! Learning the language of both is a complete asset. Much later down the road what I had discovered was a front seat to observe, to listen and to respond to the qualities of both. Maybe I did not always respond in a gentle manner, but I knew something most never come to learn. Everyone will have friendships and will have relationships no matter the size or popularity within their social circles. All our relationship encounters will appear different in comparison to anothers. Some are meant to transform us, and some are strictly like a derailed business transaction. The ones that transform us will be of great service for our now and our future. The derailed business transaction will want you to serve it if you are not careful. The one that is meant to transform you into the image of Christ will not always be the popular choice. The one that is the popular choice can sometimes distort Christ's true image.

Do not beat yourself down about either choice you make. Both will serve for transformation in all areas of growth. Open yourself up to take in the snippet of advice and run with your own crowd. The popular crowd is in Heaven!

FINAL WORD: I pray that you are set free from feeling undiscovered in Jesus name, Amen.

A FORWARD MOVING INFLUENCE

DAY 48

So Christ has truly set us free. Now make sure that you stay free, and don't get tied up again in slavery to the law.

— *GALATIANS 5:1 NLT*

We must be aware of the influence we have on generations yet to come. Please do not shut the book when I say the word electronics, we have fifty-two more days left to let me eat these words. The world of electronics is like one big bad word. Today I feel like putting the word to rest, along with every device sucking the life out of future generations. Firmly standing on my personal belief, they do serve a purpose. For instance, I am writing to you every day on one now.

Parenting comes with a long laundry list of all the dos, and all don'ts. Where I have been hostage, my children will feel freedom. We inspire examples and even help forge a path for them. Someday they will walk out of our homes with implements to apply into their own homes. If you are saying I do not have children so this must not be for me and are trying to skip ahead wait! Do not believe that lie, the world is clocked in my friend and the eyes are upon all of us. In grocery lines, restaurants, gyms, parks, the eyes peer everywhere. We make jokes that electronics are today's handheld babysitters for parents, but are they not our personal babysitters as well? We wait at the doctor's office, dentist or checkout lines and what is the first thing we reach for? For me personally, it is not a magazine or communication with a patron.

I am not sharing this with you to say do without. I share to say we can all do better. What might we be modeling to those we may never lift our eyes to see looking back to us? Again, electronics have become essential to completing many tasks in our day, but there is still a way to positively influence future generations. What might you be prematurely exposing generations to around you? Dismantling old behaviors just may be the freedom train headed down a whole new set of tracks.

FINAL WORD: I pray scales upon eyes be removed in Jesus' name, Amen.

ARMORED

DAY 49

*Because of this, you must wear all the armor that God provides so you're
protected as you confront the slanderer, for you are destined for all things
and will rise victorious. Put on truth as a belt to strengthen you to stand
in triumph. Put on holiness as the protective armor that covers your
heart. Stand on your feet alert, then you'll always be ready to share the
blessings of peace. In every battle, take faith as your wrap-around shield,
for it is able to extinguish the blazing arrows coming at you from the
Evil One! Embrace the power of salvation's full deliverance, like a
helmet to protect your thoughts from lies. And take the mighty razor-
sharp Spirit-sword of the spoken Word of God. Pray passionately in the
Spirit, as you constantly intercede with every form of prayer at all times.
Pray the blessings of God upon all his believers. And pray also that
God's revelation would be released through me every time I preach the
wonderful mystery of the hope-filled gospel.*

— EPHESIANS 6:13-19 TPT

I n the book Ephesians the Apostle Paul left some
recorded lines. The Passion Translation breaks
these verses down into detailed solutions for
everyday battles. On a more personal note, today I would

like to share a story that has helped me picture what the Apostle Paul was trying to describe to the world in his letter.

Our youngest boy asked to play baseball in an organized league. After a few practices the position determined for him was catcher. Sitting in the stands as supportive parents in ninety-degree weather, I began to admire the way he suited up each game. At one point during the season I asked him, "Do you not grow weary of suiting up several times during the game?" In the sweetest little boy response he said, "No ma'am it is so fun!"

Taking inventory of all the individual parts required before walking on the field, I was reminded of Apostle Paul's instruction. Every day on earth, walking with God is meant to be fun. How could we possibly obtain that kind of fun for our own lives then? Each day we are given is essentially played out on God's ballfield. Should we not also be suited up in full armor before stepping foot on the field? If we are choosing to play ball on Team God, then we will always have an opposing team we are up against (the enemy). I want the opposing team to say when they see me walk on the field, "Oh no, she's here!" Get to your dugout and suit yourself with your full armor. Get suited beloved, your team is depending on you.

FINAL PRAYER: I pray that you suit up with the belt of truth, the breastplate of righteousness, tie your shoes with peace, put on the helmet of salvation and carry your sword of the Spirit, Amen.

WHERE IS YOUR FOCUS?

DAY 50

And the King will say, 'I tell you the truth, when you did it to one of the least of these my brothers and sisters, you were doing it to me!'

— *MATTHEW 25:40 NLT*

For the last few years, some women and I who attend our church have come together each November for a craft night. The focus surrounding this special event is to put together no-sew blankets to be donated locally to our food bank. No-sew fleece blankets are constructed of two yards cut separately, of two different patterns of fleece, with all the edges tied in knots holding it together. Generally, we have a great turnout of women who participate from all over the county making this event a wonderful success. The evening is so rewarding as we fellowship and move from blanket to blanket helping each other tie knots to complete them before the night's end. At the end of the night, we circle together hand in hand surrounding these blankets stacked high and pray over them before sending them forth.

We are always so excited to see returning faces and new ones for this event. The evening is opened by explaining the focus of the event and where these blankets have gone in the past and will be going in the future. There is always the option that anyone who attended and brought their own material can keep the blanket they worked hard on. We also make it clear that if they do not feel led to give the blanket they should not. By the end of the night, my mind is always blown at what we see as the women all walk out empty-handed. The only words that come to my mind to express the excitement over the event is "Go God." These women come through these doors with full hands of fabric and walk away with a focus for giving back to the Kingdom.

In Matthew we are told how important it is to feed, to clothe, and to care for the needs of the less fortunate. We are instructed in the word of the importance of doing this. When we perform these acts of kindness, we are performing as hands and feet for Jesus and bringing great honor for our King. Will you or have you now become inspired to do the things that you have been wanting to do? Give back to a need and your spirit will thank you for it! In the smallest or largest acts of kindness remember you are doing it for King Jesus!

FINAL WORD: I pray that whatever that thing is you have always wanted to do for another that today it becomes action, Amen.

NOTHING IN NATURE BLOOMS
ALL YEAR

DAY 51

We are pressed on every side by troubles, but we are not crushed. We are perplexed, but not driven to despair. We are hunted down, but never abandoned by God. We get knocked down, but we are not destroyed. Through suffering, our bodies continue to share in the death of Jesus so that the life of Jesus may also be seen in our bodies.

— *2 CORINTHIANS 4:8-10 NLT*

Nothing in nature blooms all year. Nature is full of beautiful flowers but even they have a time for radiating their beauty through blooms. Reveal to me flowers that continue to bloom as their best vibrant self all year? Only after it has had time to let the old die off does it return to its true nature. I want to invite you into a safe place today to sit with the Father and ask Him to take you deeper into areas that may have caused you to stay stuck or maybe you currently are stuck. Before you read further about things that have held me captive personally, I invite you to ask the Lord to show you places that your flesh has held you captive. Allow the Lord to show you a different way to see hope in those areas and invite Him in to allow the places to die off. If you're ready, I am certainly ready, so let us begin!

When we are forgotten, uninvited, uncelebrated yet know we are remembered by the Father, we have died to self. When our input and ideas carry little influence, but we are still grounded to move forth, we have died to self. When we no longer keep record of good works followed by selfish praise or our comforts are undiscovered, we have died to self. When the sound of rejoicing drowns the echoes of envy, we have died to self. Acquiring little, having a lot, mingling with the rich or mingling with the poor. When correction submits to the authority of humility, we have died to self.

In forward movement with God, we will have a lifetime of opportunity to bring beauty into the places that were lifeless. Second to receiving the eternal gift of Salvation, the Holy Spirit's everlasting gift to all is to guide us forever. The Holy Spirit will guide, guard and protect us over all areas as we allow the old flesh to lay down in areas that once caused everlasting concern. Christ's perfect image is the reflection of the dead things turned to resurrected beauty. Allow vulnerability today to complete the work in you. To be in a place demonstrating His best work, you must allow Him to have access into every place.

FINAL WORD: I pray that you are motivated with help from the Holy Spirit to let go the dead things of the flesh, Amen.

PRAISE TO THE HEAVENS ABOVE

DAY 52

Let every created thing give praise to the LORD, for he issued his command, and they came into being.

— *PSALM 148:5 NLT*

Witnessing the sun as it crests over the horizon in the wee early hours of the morning is how I enjoy partnering with the new day. Stepping out into the crisp morning air to get a much closer view and feel of His glorious creation allows me to take it all into my entire being. The smells of the dew in the morning air, the taste of the freedom escaping in and out of my lungs, and the sounds of nature raising their voices to the light breaking through the dark. Everything in creation raises a praise to the heavens above at this time of day. As the morning sun rises everything has opportunity to witness the invitation and participate in this magnificent event.

I can feel the longing in your spirit now to partner with the morning. Take a moment and reflect on a classic

Disney movie with me that most everyone has seen called *Bambi*. The light of the morning awakens life within a forest and all creation celebrates with shouts of joy. This is how I picture the light of the morning across the entire world even though I cannot see from one end to the other. I imagine myself a tree in the forest and its many creations waiting for that first breath of light to peak, to catch the experience of God's creation coming to life. What a knockout, stand-up job God allows us to experience each day!

Start simple, start small, set an alarm tomorrow morning for just before sunrise, and with all senses tuned in, take direct notice of just the birds singing the praises at first. Listen for just their responses echoing to nature, catch the sounds of nature's vibrations in the air. If tomorrow nothing else brings joy streaming in, make an appointment with the praise of all creation. Your mind, body and soul will thank you for it.

FINAL WORD: I pray for an encounter with all His creation, Amen.

PRAY UNTIL

DAY 53

Jesus replied, "But even more blessed are all who hear the word of God and put it into practice."

— *LUKE 11:28 NLT*

P ray not until God hears, but until you listen to God! A testimony of words that are living hope. Giving over my life to Christ sparked a new fire within. I was on a mission to share my new friend Jesus with all. Whenever, wherever and with whomever, I may have been a bit overbearing about approaching this subject in my home, workplace or store. Receiving fresh revelations each time I spent time in God's presence and word, I often found myself spilling over. My family, often the main target, would respond with "can we talk about anything else?" In response I would take no such advice.

What was meant for good backfired into something bad, becoming a bitter root in my loved ones. While I was so busy fanning my own flame within, it was beginning to extinguish the flame of others. One evening my husband shared something with me that forever took root and grew. He shared a childhood story with me about growing up and having the pleasure of riding racehorses. This was not at all something new to me, so I slightly turned a deaf ear to this conversation. Next he told me that their family intentionally used blinders now and again on the eyes of the horse, explaining that this was not to intentionally blind the horse but to encourage them to focus forward and to run their own race. Tuning back in immediately to him he now asked me this question, "Would you consider pacing yourself in the pack, allowing the blinders to slightly come down and look around please?" In response I obliged and instantly heard the Lord say, "everyone will have an opportunity to get where I have planned for them."

Not just the words from my beloved husband but the Father's words helped me to realize that I may have been throwing mud in the eyes of others unintentionally. God has a race for me to finish and win, he does not have me winning a race for everyone in the pack. Out in the lead is not always the place to be. Sometimes falling to the back of the pack you gain the ground needed to win the race.

FINAL WORD: *I pray you know that you are doing great at your own speed and your own race, just continue to run, Amen.*

I EXALT THEE

DAY 54

I will exalt you, my God and King, and praise your name forever and ever.

— *PSALM 145:1 NLT*

What does the word exalt even mean, right? Let us take the word exalt and explore it for a moment. By Webster's definition exalt is to raise in rank, power, or character; to elevate by praise or to glorify.[1] Now that we cleared that up let me ask you what receives the highest rank, power, or praise in your life at the moment? Is it your spouse, a boyfriend or girl-friend, your parents? Your children, your career, your finances? Home, cars, boats, RV, horses, cows or the trips you take or do not get to take?

It is perfectly normal if you chose "All of the above." Answering yes to one or more of these brings us in common with one another. See, we know way more about each other than we thought. The definition of exalt is seen as something having place above all else, for instance, taking top rank above all else in our lives. Other than the One true God, there is nothing that truly deserves to be exalted or glorified more. Before I lose all attention of the reader, hearing the harsh reality in order to reposition God at the center of all is a good thing not a judgement.

Anything that we choose to exalt or put on the throne above God will eventually be dethroned. The things that once ranked having control or power higher than God like my own accomplishments or my personal friendships are no longer in my possession. Why? Not because I tried to relinquish those areas over to God freely. I wish today you could be reading a different story of how I did it all on my own. No, it was because whatever entered my hands I had a habit of turning into a possession, placing it higher than God. Whatever will be for us will first have to pass through the precious hands of God. Is there something in your hand now that you have a death grip on that must lose power? Stop toiling with it and hand it over allowing the accomplishment to rest in the hands of King Jesus.

FINAL WORD: I pray that everything that has been exalted above God be dethroned in Jesus name, Amen.

DEAR, EVERYTHING I LOST

DAY 55

Dear brothers and sisters, when troubles come your way, consider it an opportunity for great joy.

— *JAMES 1:2 NLT*

Earlier on I touched on divorce and the idea of "broken homes." I have read that almost half of all marriages in the United States end in divorce. The number one cause reported is lack of commitment. Around the early age of twelve, my parents divorced. Early in the process of their divorce I sensed that things would never be the same again. Children who come from broken homes at young ages sometimes put much blame on their parents and experience relationships within their own life that can falter. By age twenty-two, several relationships in my immediate circle were almost extinct. By age thirty-five, what few were left were completely non-existent.

Sitting here free today, I can say to everything I have ever lost, I sincerely thank God. The agony we carry from the heartaches and losses we experience can feel so personal or leave us feeling defenseless. To every relationship or possession that thinks it owns you or has come to paralyze the best in you I speak directly to and say over you today "it must be broken from you now in the name of Jesus." Whatever was intended to harm you hear me when I say, "God intended it for good." There is a Scripture that I want you to look to and get familiar with in the book of Genesis. Joseph was recorded saying to his brothers "You meant evil against me, but God used it for good."

The traumas that happened throughout your life were not your fault and God will use them for good. The divorce you went through or were witness to God will use for good. The addiction you witnessed or fought through God will use it for good. The death of a loved one God will use it for good. Beloved, if reading these lines and they are speaking directly to you of that kind of pain, I say to you now, do not ask God to change the circumstances of the situation. Ask Him now to change you through the situation. Whatever intended to harm you, God intended it for good. Rise up in your troubles and rest in the words of Joseph: "You intended to harm me, but God intended it for good to accomplish what is now being done, the saving of many lives." (Genesis 50:20 NIV).

Bless the hand of favor that has come upon your life, to use all pain—past, present, and future—to save many others In Jesus' Name.

FINAL WORD: I pray a renewed perspective throughout every situation, Amen.

ON THE THRONE

DAY 56

God's splendor is a tale that is told; his testament is written in the stars. Space itself speaks his story every day through the marvels of the heavens. His truth is on tour in the starry vault of the sky, showing his skill in creation's craftsmanship.

— *PSALM 19:1 TPT*

Traveling long distances in the car with your parents on vacation, what do you remember having for entertainment? Wow, the days before TVs, iPads, and portable games in the car. Looking out the window in pure silence trying to make something out of clouds. Discovery can also be found in plain sight in our imagination. Well into adulthood, at least for me, not much has changed. I am still intrigued by the beautiful blue skies and puffy white clouds that dance above.

A group from our church a few years back joined in a pre-Christmas evening outing. Several attended a live performance walking us through the Bible. On the drive there, the sky was full of beautiful white puffy clouds and clear blue skies from rains earlier that day. In the far distance, we were headed into an enormous cloud formation. The cloud began to take on the shape and form of a huge crown in the sky. As it slowly built each notch of the crown extending higher and farther apart from the base of cloud, we took it in thinking that we had been the only family in the carpool that witnessed this event.

Upon arrival, among members of the group the questions flew as to who had seen the large cloud formation that looked like a crown. Several had even captured a photograph of the cloud formation. Now seated in the large outdoor amphitheater waiting for the play to begin, signs of possible rain danced above, with lightning in the distance. Storms that evening rolled in from every direction around the outdoor event center for three hours straight. Not a single drop of rain fell on anyone in attendance. God had a clear message that evening forecasted to all in the cloud formation. He had taken care of the evening right from His throne. Rejoice and trust that God is seated in attendance to handle all events.

FINAL WORD: I pray that you search out the things God writes above, Amen.

THE STRENGTH TO BREAK

DAY 57

He trains my hands for battle; he strengthens my arm to draw a bronze bow.

— *PSALM 18:34 NLT*

To get better we must allow the times, trials and all the shared experiences in life to enrich our journey. We will never experience how to bend without having experienced how to break. All will experience a break in life. Several will linger in moments figuring out how to carry on. Maybe it has already shown up in extreme health issues, a financial situation, a prodigal child, or a fractured relationship. Are you familiar with the terms short-term and long-term disability? While both provide some level of assistance during a time of need, there is a point when both will run out. Meaning that when they do it is time to seek a new plan of action. What will be the next move then?

If I can suggest to you the best course of action to take, it is always to move closer to God. The chosen term policies will not sustain all long-term breaks. Eventually we will need a source for more compensation. Can we be vulnerable and humble enough to allow God to do what it is only He can do? He is already fully aware of all the crossroads we will ever encounter. God encourages us to pull Him out of the waiting room and extend the invite. He is full of the insurance and assurance we are seeking. God is already the full coverage plan offered. Will you allow God to be the sole beneficiary?

FINAL WORD: I pray today for your ability to fully accept God's long-term coverage, Amen.

CHANGE IN SEASONS

DAY 58

For everything there is a season, a time for every activity under heaven. A time to be born and a time to die. A time to plant and a time to harvest. A time to kill and a time to heal. A time to tear down and a time to build up. A time to cry and a time to laugh. A time to grieve and a time to dance. A time to scatter stones and a time to gather stones. A time to embrace and a time to turn away. A time to search and a time to quit searching. A time to keep and a time to throw away. A time to tear and a time to mend. A time to be quiet and a time to speak. A time to love and a time to hate. A time for war and a time for peace.

— *ECCLESIASTES 3:1-8 NLT*

Seasons. What defines them and how are they woven into our own lives? In the identifying markers of nature, the appearance of one season will not mimic the appearance of another. Temperatures outside change, the amount of light and darkness change, and then the landscape changes. From summer to winter, spring to fall, the seasons are completely outside of our control. Take for instance the sun and moon, they need no directions from us to know when to set and when to rise. The crafted hands of "The Almighty Creator" are responsible for all events.

Just as this takes place around us with no special instructions, we also have these seasons designated to do the same. What about the seasons that change in our personal life? Is it too far-fetched to believe we experience seasonal changes? Let us look at childhood friendships. Probably most are not the same people in your lives today. In fact, a large majority of high school friendships are nowhere near the same either. Could you pinpoint something that caused this change? Is that possible for you? Of course not, they simply served a purpose for a time. You will frequently see seasonal transitions in your own life. Just like nature takes orders from God, you will partner in His changing of seasons as you mature in relationship with Him.

Most recently I heard the seasons of life told in a story about space shuttles. For departure to space, a shuttle is equipped with extra tanks for support. As the shuttle breaks through different altitudes into space, the extra tanks drop off. This is by design for good—they do exactly what they were intended to do at that moment. Where the shuttle was going the extra weight could not follow. Seasons come and go inviting the best lessons to be learned for life. Do not allow the extra weight to hinder you. Hard freezes are meant to assist in the new growth.

FINAL WORD: *I pray you invite the hard freezes of life in to create new growth, Amen.*

THE REASON

DAY 59

Most important of all, continue to show deep love for each other, for love covers a multitude of sins.

— *1 PETER 4:8 NLT*

G randparents versus parents? Most everyone knows of one, has or had one, or is one or will be one. From the earliest childhood memories, the word "love" was never questioned in our home. The word was used frequently in our home. The divorce of my parents had been the first example of love being any different through actions. Coping with my parent's divorce was not easy for me. In fact, it was downright difficult. What love put on display in the home suddenly just welcomed itself in as the opposite light simply overnight. Adjustments to everyday routines were sudden and rapid. Being a product of divorce, I do know that children tend to search for reasons why. Divorce simply feels as if it owes no explanation to children at all.

Divorce equals two people choosing to give up period. I feel compelled to speak on this subject because I was a product of divorce and I have fought with every bit of my living being to keep my marriage intact. Children are not afforded the same road out to freedom that a parent or grandparent has in a divorce. Please hear me, I understand in some situations there may be no other option and those come with a different set of instructions. I am solely speaking to the situations where divorce became easier than keeping the covenant made by marrying.

When two people wed, they are making a vow in front of God to love one another in the good, the bad, in the times of sickness and in health, until death do they part. Love is a choice we make and come into covenant with when we vow to partner with God. What love will do is cover a multitude of sins. This verse does not tell us to follow the multitudes of sin, nor is sin hidden behind the word love. The instruction of the verse is to show deep love for one another because, by doing so, love will be the cover over all sin. We love people out of the places of their sin, beloved. God's love and grace was enough for you. Is it enough for them?

FINAL WORD: I pray that if God's grace was enough for you then it is enough for them, Amen.

GIANTS

DAY 60

David replied to the Philistine, "You come to me with sword, spear, and javelin, but I come to you in the name of the LORD of Heaven's Armies —the God of the armies of Israel, whom you have defied. Today the LORD will conquer you, and I will kill you and cut off your head. And then I will give the dead bodies of your men to the birds and wild animals, and the whole world will know that there is a God in Israel! And everyone assembled here will know that the LORD rescues his people, but not with sword and spear. This is the LORD's battle, and he will give you to us!"

— *1 SAMUEL 17:45-47 NLT*

There is a familiar Bible story most children and even adults could recite to some degree. It is the story of David and Goliath. Recently I had the opportunity to teach this in our children's church class where I saw it with a fresh perspective. Whether boy or girl, when asked what story they would enjoy hearing the class all agreed to hear about David and Goliath. Beginning the lesson I was reading sensitively around the part where David takes off Goliath's head. The class interrupted with "you skipped the head part!"

I had continued the act of dancing around the subject then I asked each child to stand up. I had them mimic the shape of bowling pins at the end of a bowling lane. One toward the front and several following suit, one child would be left at the very back off in the distance and one at the front alone. The child asked to stand at the front would turn and deliver a kind word to each child in the path of getting to the one in the far distance (our Goliath). As the children took turns speaking kind words each would then sit down, representing the bowling ball knocking down a bowling pin. The one off in the far distance represented our Goliath. Once standing face to face with Goliath, the children were instructed to use a word, phrase or Scripture from the Bible to knock out Goliath. Each child had an opportunity to participate in each role and took great pleasure in doing so.

I had demonstrated to these children that we are each fully equipped with the power to defeat our Goliaths. The source of our power can be found in God's living word. Partake in the study and digest the power that God's word has authority to do. God's word is there for the day that your Goliath will need to be slayed!

. . .

FINAL WORD: I pray the words from your mouth go forth to slay your giants, Amen.

A CLEAN HEART

DAY 61

Create in me a clean heart, O God. Renew a loyal spirit within me.

— *PSALM 51:10 NLT*

For I was born a sinner yes, from the moment my mother conceived me (Psalm 51:5 NLT). We are all born out of broken spirit. None of us are called to stay in that place. Confession and repentance of sins before God removes guilt and renews the new man within. No matter the level of sin, God can redeem it all! Once freed of guilt and shame we are adopted into God's family. Receiving through His wisdom a new path, new thoughts and new patterns to walk in through the gift of the Holy Spirit.

Not to dismiss kingdom sons, but in addressing all kingdom daughters, I feel the urgency to remind them that they are not alone. The woman speaking these words on this page to you was just a little girl a few short years ago. Spending a lifetime believing I had been cheated out of some things that the world owed me left me stunted in my growth. The dads that coached sports, the father and daughter dates, Father's Day celebrations, and missed opportunity on a big wedding day to name a few. From the depths of wanting to be seen, known and loved, my actions were to covet what I thought others had. Not just months but years at length I built up gaps of disappointment. Outward demonstrations planted inward resentment toward all men, elevating a hardened heart and a large chip on my shoulder.

The words we speak have the power and ability to bless or to curse us. Long before I had any understanding of my future destiny, the word curses had been formed. But God showing the kind of love, attention, and hope I had always longed for and desired left me speechless. Destiny had caught up to my future and found me in the arms of my Heavenly Father full of mercy and forgiveness. All that I ever thought to be true of men left me melting in the arms of the one true man, God. I long for you to know that Our Heavenly Father fills in all the missing gaps.

FINAL WORD: I pray for a cleansed heart and a renewed spirit within, Amen.

THE CONSULTANT

DAY 62

Seek his will in all you do, and he will show you which path to take.

— *PROVERBS 3:6 NLT*

Have you ever found yourself between a rock and a hard place? Has it ever been from your mouth speaking out as your flesh rose? I think many use the more familiar phrase "Insert foot in mouth." I have experienced this several times over several things and at times still do. Moving to the state of Texas in 2004, married without children, we were living our best life— or so my husband and I thought. We were caught up in chasing all the things couples think are desirable to sustain and fulfill life. The first homes, extra cars, motorcycles, boats and well you get the point, stuff period. Great paying jobs allow great expenses, so let us get familiar with the phrase "you make more money, you just spend more money." As a couple we nailed down the art of consulting with one another and our friends. This was disappointing to say the least, not because those friends did assist, but because we chose to mirror their lifestyles.

Why in the world did we copy behaviors? The flesh wanted what others had, that is why. Consulting with God, our true business partner, never crossed our minds, not once. Within five short years of marriage, we were pregnant with our first son and looking forward to starting a family. The bottom started falling out of our careers and luxury choices. We had hit a pivotal turning point in our lives and were ready to prioritize who we would be consulting with. The perfect suitor was no one other than God.

Take the example of choosing the right realtor to negotiate a suitable home purchase, price, and location for your family. Choosing the right team member is crucial for all future endeavors. Every move you make should be made with God the primary consultant.

FINAL WORD: I pray that God has been consulted first and last, Amen.

SCRATCH YOUR BACK

DAY 63

I am leaving you with a gift—peace of mind and heart. And the peace I give is a gift the world cannot give. So don't be troubled or afraid.

— *JOHN 14:27 NLT*

Great pleasure rests in the hands of a horse owner. Many have been quoted saying that you will never own the horse, the vet bills will. Arguing this statement would be a laughing matter. Large amounts of fear surround the thoughts of people, horse and rider. On another note, many have encountered the horse and found instant love for the animal.

Surprisingly, I have personally fallen on both sides of the fence of this discussion. Spending most of my summers riding every single day with friends I developed into a seasoned rider. Experiencing incidents of falling off, I would get right back on. Small accidents never kept me much paralyzed in fear but rather made me watch each step.

Observing horses through the years of growing up gave me the opportunity to study horse behavior. Known to be a highly social herd animal, horses enjoy companionship. In forming companionship among the herd the horse demonstrates the same behaviors as humans. The horse, if isolated from the herd, can become anxious. Another common behavior is that the horse is a fight or flight species. Although horse lovers have removed most of the predators from the presence of the horse, they are born with this instinct. The first instinct of the horse when fear sets in is to escape, also known as the flight instinct. If not able to escape they may resort to biting, kicking, stomping and rearing.

Now with that overview, I invite you to examine some of our own behaviors. Do we seek companionship? Yes! We sure do and we were designed for fellowship. Does fear lead us to demonstrate the fight and flight behaviors at times? Yes, familiar experiences can cause us to fight or to take flight. God's design was for us to run in companionship with Him. Look back to the beginning—the story in Genesis of Adam and Eve. When cornered what did Eve do? She took the bite. Rest assured, we have all been here. What might be that one thing that corners you? Know that God is for you, ahead of you and will never leave you. God desires for you to commune in His herd.

FINAL WORD: I pray for your fight and flight mentality accepting the conditions that God is for you, Amen.

SUNFLOWER

DAY 64

We are glad to seem weak if it helps show that you are actually strong.
We pray that you will become mature.

— *2 CORINTHIANS 13:9 NLT*

Within a month of purchasing of our new home five years ago, my husband was laid off. The company he had been employed with was not willing to give full disclosure of the layoff, but the severance package offered was explanation enough. We knew we had prayed with fervent hearts to God over our new home purchase and we also knew clearly that we heard Him to move forward in the purchase. What we also were certain about was that even though the storm raged currently overhead, the SON was still present. While it was devastating nonetheless, we would still follow and trust God.

Every morning still joyful and counting it all joy we marched on. As the weeks passed, I found myself leaving my three guys at home. For three full months my husband stepped into the role of stay-at-home parent, caring for our two young boys while I cared for the other needs to be met. Praying continuously for God's helping hand over our situation the silence became deafening. Drawing to the end of the three month mark and the severance hours away from expiring, the answer was delivered to us in less than twenty-four hours.

At a local restaurant my husband sat in an interview with a well-established owner of an oil company. Surpassing all our understanding, he was hired on the spot and would become a top asset to the rapidly growing company. This new position allowed more freedom to be a father to our boys and a husband to me. God is the manager, the boss, and the overseer of closing certain doors tight. God has great intent for the greater in store. Can you still draw praise from your situation? God assures us that our problems will not have ownership of us, they will become the place to mature us.

FINAL WORD: I pray every storm you may come to know that the SON still shines, Amen.

DO NOT LET ME MISS THIS

DAY 65

Anyone who listens to my teaching and follows it is wise, like a person who builds a house on solid rock. Though the rain comes in torrents and the floodwaters rise and the winds beat against that house, it won't collapse because it is built on bedrock.

— *MATTHEW 7:24-25 NLT*

Wife and mother can contend with each other for first place. Not for one second would I ever trade one role for the other. Becoming a wife was hardly something I had dreamed of. Early childhood examples hindered that a bit. But thankfully here I am, proudly rocking it right along with motherhood. Every single moment has not been good but everything good has come from every moment.

On the topic of marriage, let us not argue the fact that it can be one of the hardest things you will walk through. Add a few little ones to the equation and you just doubled if not tripled the difficulty level. Reality is double that per kiddo added to the family. Not really, okay really, your grocery bill just doubled, fuel expenses, health insurance more than doubled and along came new child-care expenses. On a more serious note, the real struggle rears its ugly head when two working parents ask one another who will drop off and who will pick up today? Better yet, how can we be at two places at once? How about the most talked over question, "when will there be time for just the two of us?" Believe me when I say you are so not alone.

Whether your mother, grandmother, closest friends, closest relative or closest enemy wants to admit it, this is the struggle of balancing both roles. For several years, my home felt like it was in complete and total chaos. Quite honestly it took a friend of the truest kind to sit me down and help me recognize chaos. Delivered with gentle compassion, those words still ring like music to my ears. Informed that if my home was not in order, the rest of my world would not be in order. The word tells us to build our home on solid rock. When the rains come, the floodwaters rise, and wind beats against our home it will not collapse because of the bedrock it stands on. The point? It might be time to examine our foundation. Is your home structurally sound on the Word of God?

FINAL WORD: I pray that you prepare your homes on the bedrock, Amen.

LEAVE ONLY FOOTPRINTS

DAY 66

Your path led through the sea, your way through the mighty waters,
though your footprints were not seen.

— *PSALM 77:19 NIV*

During a recent vacation at the beach, my family and I had a great opportunity to experience more of the relationship side of God. What is it about the beach that draws us a little closer to Heaven? Wild guess but it could be the warmth, the tiny grains of sand, the repeated sounds of crashing waves or the sweet sounds of families at play. Once you get still in a place like that you cannot help but draw closer to the presence of God.

Each morning took us on a path across a two-lane road onto the boardwalk leading to the endless grains of sand. Before stepping foot on the beach, we would drop our shoes below the sign at the boardwalk that said, "LEAVE ONLY FOOTPRINTS." Our daily billboard got me thinking about footprints with God.

Just days after my trip in my weekly Bible study group, the same question had been up for discussion. The author of the book talked about when we got to Heaven, we might have similar questions like this to ask of God, retracing all our steps together with Him on earth. Now I am not going to be able to quote it verbatim, I am just going to try to paint a picture of the reading. We may ask the questions along the lines of who the second set of footprints were along with ours? God may inform us that His were the consistent ones and ours were not. We might even ask God where He might have been headed? In response to us, "the plans I had just designed specifically for you." Then we might ask where were mine? The answer: "Headed back the other way picking up old ways and choosing opposite pathways." He might even share that we were never abandoned during the times we abandoned Him, heading off in our own direction. We might choose to ask why we stopped so often? God might say, "It was about what you were willing to surrender child." Then the moment may come when we say, "God but am I here with you now in Heaven." God, the compassionate Father replies with "of course you are here."

Taking one last glance back where once we walked, glancing at all the footprints in the sand asking God a final question: "What are all those beautifully wrapped presents left along the pathway?" In reply, He shares that all of those were just for you my child from me my beloved, precious child. Continuing the walk, He shares how all the open ones are the ones received as we walked the same pathways. The closed ones represent when we walked apart. Beloved, the obedience of pairing with God will bring us into one set of footprints.

. . .

FINAL WORD: I pray the pairing of paths with God bringing you into one set of footprints, Amen.

THAT FRIEND

DAY 67

If one person falls, the other can reach out and help. But someone who falls alone is in real trouble.

— *ECCLESIASTES 4:10 NLT*

Having a huge heart for animals sometimes gets me the title of borderline hoarder. Have you ever watched the television show on hoarders? It is a real thing and I believe we all have a slight tendency to overindulge our lifestyle with an abundance of desirable things. Perhaps these tendencies started out small but continued to grow through the feeling it continuously gave while obtaining more. I sure am not the one to judge on this topic because I know the depths of the places I had ventured into trying to fill deep voids within.

The animals on our place sometimes seem better fed than my family does at times. A recent incident happened this past Father's Day on our home place. Sunday mornings are often hectic as we all scramble to get off to church while the enemy tiptoes around trying to keep us home. Pulling out of the drive one Sunday morning, we took one last glance at the pasture to count the animals. We noticed and were alarmed because on twenty-five acres usually all our animals do not bunch together like what we were witnessing. Appearing off in the distance we had a horse lying down.

We turned around and got out of the vehicle and reached the area on foot. Our older horse seemed to have been down most of the night. Horses are prone to colic (also known as a terrible tummy ache) and if left untreated, it can lead to death. Pretty quickly realizing that we were at that point, called the vet.

Hard situations still have the peace of God hidden within. Noticeably, the other pasture animals gathered in a group and clearly had kept night watch over this one horse, keeping the predators away. During the final moments of the vet arriving and the horse leaving us, our other horses and donkeys stood over, gently licking her clean. I honestly have never seen this form of compassion and mourning recorded between large animals. Who might your pasture running mates be? Will they lend help in the depths of those hard places? These types of friends will be your armor when your armor is down!

FINAL WORD: I pray that God sends friendships willing to hold up your armor, Amen.

PEACE

DAY 68

Then you will experience God's peace, which exceeds anything we can understand. His peace will guard your hearts and minds as you live in Christ Jesus.

— *PHILIPPIANS 4:7 NLT*

The Word of God offers us instruction into a place of peace with God that transcends all understanding. What exactly is the meaning of the word peace? When we have freedom from disturbances, and we enter tranquility.

The Apostle Paul was credited with writing at least thirteen letters in the New Testament. Within the Old Testament and New Testament "peace" is written at least four hundred and twenty times in the King James version. Peace is a key given to us from God characterized in God and a quality of God. Also known the third of nine fruits of the Spirit, we are to acquire peace. What requirements are needed to experience peace that exceeds all understanding?

Acquiring peace may not always be simple but a dose of humility and a sprinkle of courage to believe is a good start. The humbled who remain postured within the spirit will see the peace of God, completely putting all selfishness aside. When we allow ourselves to believe and trust God is for us and not against us, the measure of faith beyond our own understanding begins to rise. When we allow God, the wheel, to take full control then we become nothing more than the passenger following the tracks of God's path.

Riding as passenger, we often do not have to put much worry or thought into the path we need to take as much as the driver does. Believing in where we are headed and having peace about it, it is much more comfortable in the passenger seat. As passenger we are obliged to set aside the importance of our own paths taken and become settled with the acquired understanding of how we got there. As we grow in knowledge of this peace as passengers through paths and experiences, we witness God at peace and that goodness washes over us. Time will always allow opportunities to count on peace and demonstrate the peace of God. Guard your hearts and minds as you live out your lives as a passenger with Christ Jesus.

FINAL WORD: I pray freed up hands from the wheel and allowances for Jesus to take the wheel, Amen.

THE MOTH

DAY 69

Don't store up treasures here on earth, where moths eat them and rust destroys them, and where thieves break in and steal. Store your treasures in heaven, where moths and rust cannot destroy, and thieves do not break in and steal. Wherever your treasure is, there the desires of your heart will also be.

— *MATTHEW 6:19-21 NLT*

What was it like visiting your great grandparent's home growing up? Mine could have been quite similar to yours maybe. Do the closets and cupboards come to my mind? The dishware and stovetop? The living room furniture? Maybe the artwork hanging along the hallways? Closets! It was the closets! Not just one closet either. I can think back to three. It was interesting each visit appeared to match the outfit seen previous times before. The purses, the shoes and the clothes all had a theme. Was playing dress up with in-style belongings a thing for you? Intrigued mostly in the sense of style that ranged from blue jean baby to warm up joggers, all the way to dress slacks and blouses (that word "blouses" how can I ever forget?). The scent of moth balls mixed with the warm aroma of clean linens starched with a spritz of yesterday's perfume. Moth balls served a purpose, I guess you could say, or at least they were overly convincing. These little white pesticide balls were considered damage control.

In Matthew, we are all instructed to not store up for ourselves treasures on earth, where the moth and rust destroy and where thieves break in and steal. Unfortunately, I had fallen victim to this storing up. Our hearts will follow in pursuit after whatever our eyes desire. Never will there be enough of the little white balls in our closets to keep the thieves away. Bankrupting your stockpiles in Heaven are not worth the wealth of material goods on earth.

What will you sort out of your closets today? Wherever your treasure is, there the desires of your heart will also be. I challenge you to a heavenly stockpile!

FINAL WORD: I pray over your heavenly stockpile and that all your storehouses become full, Amen.

THANKSGIVING

DAY 70

Enter his gates with thanksgiving; go into his courts with praise. Give thanks to Him and praise His name.

— *PSALM 100:4 NLT*

Encouraged by Thanksgiving around the corner I was inspired to examine my gate (my mouth) of giving thanks. Easily I can get into the rut around this time of year of hanging out in pity periods, enjoying a great heaping plate piled high with complaints. The more dished out, the more likely I am to return for seconds and even thirds. How easy it is to find the least of great things in each day rather than search out and find the greatest. Just a few years back someone shared something with me that I successfully implemented in my daily life.

I purchased my first ever five-year journaling ledger. This ledger is designed with five lines for entries, on each day of the year, over a five-year period. I used to record thoughts, dreams, prayers, thanksgivings, daily encounters, things to change, or just about anything you would like to dump out at the end of each day. At first, I thought it unlikely that I would stay committed and be able to create an accountability regiment. Starting small, I allowed myself to just write three things to be thankful for or to dump out before bed each day. That became an extremely helpful tool that allowed me to start somewhere. At the time, all entries seemed to be flowing easily. The days passed easily the first then the second year, but when the third year came, my recordings began to feel a bit taxing. The main reason was the pressure I put on myself to try not to duplicate the things I was thankful or not so thankful for in the entries recorded. In my search for new things in each day to record, I overworked my thought process trying to stay mindful of avoiding duplication of yesterday's entry.

Have you ever heard how all your yesterdays transform your tomorrows? Transformation can only be celebrated after reflecting on the past and allowing it to be the lost company of the present. Some of my entries were the helpline my heart needed to see. The duplicated recordings of rejection and bitterness turned to disappointment. The negative entries helped jump start the tune in my ears to listen more and come in agreement less.

In doing these journal entries long enough, I caught on to my patterns that bled onto these pages. If the pages were inked with patterns of negativity, then the same sound echoed from my mouth. I was now in the know and assured that the sound that I wanted to come in companionship with was focused through the lens of all the goodness of God.

I have read that to form a new behavior, it takes roughly sixty-six days; to break an old behavior, it only takes twenty-one days. Journal your way into the courts of thanksgiving by living less out of past habit and more intentionally in the moment!

FINAL WORD: I pray you begin the breaking of the old and forming of the new, Amen.

EXCITEMENT

DAY 71

For I know the plans I have for you, says the LORD. They are plans for good and not for disaster, to give you a future and a hope.

— *JEREMIAH 29:11 NLT*

While flipping through a book recently I came across this statement from an unknown source: "Things that excite you are not random, they are connected to your purpose, follow them!"[1] Stepping out of high school, eighteen and clueless about my future, a lifelong career was the furthest thing from my mind. I had only three years work experience during high school. I had brief conversations with school counselors and one or maybe two college tours ever. Finishing a degree beyond high school was nothing more than a pipe dream.

Scholarships were part of the high school work experience program I had been enrolled in and I had only attended those meetings so I could escape from the school campus by fourth period. The teacher (the same teacher my parents had in high school) strongly encouraged everyone in the program to apply for any and every scholarship available. The majority of my work experience obtained by eighteen was all in customer service. I worked in lots of customer service jobs such as food service, tanning booth receptionist, private investigation receptionist, vet assistant, dog grooming assistant, and dairy farm equipment parts runner. None of the jobs I held were related to connecting with my God-given purpose, or so I had thought.

Leaving high school with a few scholarships in hand I was persuaded to try EMT school with hopes of later becoming a paramedic. I used up every bit of scholarship money I was awarded and every bit of savings I had put back through working after only about two months. I was then deemed a college dropout. Depleted financially and in need of replenishment, I found myself right back in the arms of food service by day and tanning booth receptionist at night. Late one evening as I sat at work a patron shared with me the details of a cosmetology program. They told me that in a year I could be in and out of school and make a good living. The thought of independent work, fast cash, and a profitable living—this sounded great for me or any eighteen-year old. Within weeks I was enrolled and accepted into the cosmetology program. Attending the full-time day program allowed me to have a fulltime evening and weekend job. After a year of fast-track education, I was now holding a state of California cosmetology license. Far from the idea of fast cash and independent scheduling, I was left sitting with cost of rent and product and in complete despair.

Beginning work I initially had hours without clients while those around me spun around one after another in their chairs. I began to really question my decision. The thought of going back into food service as my future was looking a little too probable for comfort. There were long periods of growth both emotionally and physically, I was developing, and often had days of feeling jealous, insecure and defeated. Learning how to persevere through something is sometimes the exact place we find our future purpose.

Several times throughout my career others in my chair have reminded my soul of this. If you are blessed enough to wake up each day doing what it is you love doing, then you are fortunate to have never worked a day in your life. I am the fortunate one then my friend! It is okay not to know the plans God has for you. But know that God still has your specific plan. The plans God has for you are for good and will not harm you. The plans will give you a future and hope. Remember the things that excite you most are not random they are connected to your purpose. Now go follow them!

FINAL WORD: I pray for your purpose to come forth, Amen.

DO NOT GIVE UP

DAY 72

But as for you, be strong and courageous, for your work will be rewarded.

— *2 CHRONICLES 15:7 NLT*

This past Christmas the struggles I had documented through many individual conversations now entered through my own front door. It was a silly question about what to get the kids this holiday season now that they are much older. Both my husband and I were firm believers and evenly yoked on the true meaning of Christmas being the gift of Jesus. We still celebrated Christmas with the children and left a few gifts under the tree, but we tried hard to keep it aligned with the soul's purpose.

Our interests as adults change often as do children's and this particular year their tastes transitioned from the old blocks and Legos into the high dollar handheld electronic games. In our home we are far from being the family that has all the latest electronics simply because we live in the country where Wi-Fi is very sketchy and expensive. In our youths both my husband and I did a lot of growing up in the outdoors caring for the animals on our place. In the present, now in our own home, my husband and I try to encourage the same for our children.

Far from the wishlist our children had written on the letters to Santa in misspelled and crooked lettering, my husband and I decided to create a mini ninja warrior ropes course. Searching our property we found the perfect set of trees to handle the rope course. Along with this Christmas gift, we as parents did not want them to miss the entire outdoor experience so we included a morning scavenger hunt. Our children would need to search and find their Christmas gift. Christmas morning delivered heavy fog and rain and eight clues with stops. After intense hunting and a list of clues leading in circles, our children finally found the course.

The paths we choose for ourselves can bring us several degrees of obstacles. Along the path there may be steps or alterations that are needed to stay on course. Obstacles are never meant to keep us in a position of continuous stumbling. Are you one to seek out a good challenge? Hang on to the ropes in your course and keep going. Somewhere, someone else is depending on the outcome of your obstacle.

FINAL WORD: I pray for your courage that will lead you to see the outcome, Amen.

LIGHT

DAY 73

Your eye is a lamp that provides light for your body. When your eye is good, your whole body is filled with light. But when it is bad, your body is filled with darkness.

— *LUKE 11:34 NLT*

Passing through this world we often gather many things of light and many things of dark along the way. Do you believe in having less of what does not matter and more of what does? How many friends, family, co-workers and ourselves from time to time say things along the lines of, "if I only had this, how much better off I would be?" If only I could have, if only I should have, and if only I would have. Growing up this statement was thrown around in all circles I surrounded myself with.

I was always completely clothed, fed and had a roof over my head. What was it I could have needed so much more of? For one thing it was this lost feeling deep within, struggling to find contentment. Wholeheartedly I was caught up in the belief that if only I had what my friends had my light would shine as bright or possibly brighter. Boy, howdy, how so very wrong was that lie straight from the pits of hell. Having received one nice thing, I was taking it with one hand and already waiting with the other hand extended expecting more.

Light will open the understanding of our hearts revealing what has been hidden in the dark all along. Light can be found and invited into those deep dark places through the reading of the Bible. Has something taken over the power of allowing the light in? God's word says your eye is a lamp that provides light for your body. When your eye is good, your whole body is filled with light. But when it is bad, your body is filled with darkness (Luke 11:34 NLT).

Our eyes act like an absorbing sponge. We give our eyes permission to allow the outside world to enter into our hearts. When our eyes are open to receive things of light like the truth of God's word we allow the shades to be drawn up. When the shades come up the light can enter and illuminate a room. When our eyes are closed to the things of light (only what the world wants us to believe) the shades are drawn down, allowing darkness to penetrate in areas where light intends to live. Open the windows of your heart to the word of God and allow the light to shine in!

FINAL WORD: I pray the rays of light to penetrate any area of darkness upon your hearts, Amen.

THE LEPER

DAY 74

As Jesus continued on toward Jerusalem, he reached the border between Galilee and Samaria. As he entered a village there, ten lepers stood at a distance, crying out, "Jesus, Master, have mercy on us!"

— *LUKE 17:11-13 NLT*

A re you stranded in the village, in despair, crying out for mercy? Fast forward to the scene that takes place in Luke 17:11-17. Jesus was on his way to Jerusalem when he reached the border of Galilee and Samaria. On the border Scripture says Jesus entered a village. Galilee was a place where the Jews and Gentiles mixed among one another. Galilee was home to Jesus most of his boyhood years. Most of the disciples that followed Jesus were also from Galilee. Galilee was home to many of Jesus' miracles along with some of the parables he spoke about.

I have pondered why Jesus had entered this village heading toward His past to begin with. All through the word Jesus had purposed appointments with the rejected and the outcast. Reading further on, the village Jesus stopped at was without name, leading me to believe that these ten lepers were not really the outcasts in the village off in the distance. Though the village in Scripture was without name and entirely hidden off the map, it was not off the radar to Jesus.

Imagine the scene if you will of ten lepers who stood off in the distance and cried out, recognizing Jesus and even calling Him Master pleading for mercy. Leprosy was a contagious disease causing skin pigmentation loss and was clearly visible to all if you had it. These ten men, whether knowing it or not, found themselves communing in bondage together. Pause a moment with me. How often do we choose others in our inner circles to commune with because of our likeness? God loves the outcasts; in fact he takes great pride in showing up for the outcasts. These men could have just stayed out at a distance like they had day after day. Everything was different on this day compared to any other day they had encountered before. The ten lepers had hearts in a posture of desperation. Crying out to God they said, "Jesus, Master, have mercy on us!" When they chose to use the word Master, they were informing Jesus that they knew Him and were ready to enter the "in crowd." The word confirms that Jesus looked at them and said, "Go, show yourselves to the priests." Side note: Jesus saw them and gave one set of instructions "Go, show your-selves to the priests." That was all Jesus did!

To enter in the presence of the priests you must have been spotless and appear healed to return to the crowd. Jesus was so confident that by the time they got to the priest they would indeed be healed. The story reports only one returned to Jesus praising Him for the healing received. All were made well, but the one who returned to Jesus to show gratitude was made whole. What is holding you back from the one set of instructions you have been given? Our answer, the one that makes us "whole" might possibly be in that one instruction of obedience.

FINAL WORD: *I pray that you start back at the last thing God instructed you to do and you do that thing, Amen.*

BOUNDARIES

DAY 75

Then He said to the disciples, "It is impossible that no offenses should come, but woe to him through whom they do come!"

— *LUKE 17:1 NKJV*

Our home and acreage are surrounded with barbed wire fencing. Others may be more familiar with having a fenced-in yard. Either term serves a purpose meaning to keep something in or bound to one area or to confine an area with boundaries. I recently read how barbed wire fencing can be dated back to the 1860's.

Large movements were taking place across the plains and ranchers and farmers were beginning to settle the plains shortly after the American Civil War. Ranchers and farmers were moving out on the plains and were seeking a way to fence off portions for safe keeping of their live-stock. Wood and stone were much too expensive to be of use. A cost-effective solution came in the form of the barbed wire fence. I want to direct my question from the fence on to you. How does the word "confinement" sit in your spirit?

Having had many encounters with barbed wire fencing, there are proper protocols for handling. Gloves and long sleeve clothing are required. Not easily maneuvered through, over or even under, it is well known for its number one characteristic—razor sharp barbs that rip and tear clothing and skin.

While recently studying about Luke in 17:1 "offense" is something that we are told to refrain from. Offense in relation to a barbed wire fence will keep us restricted or stuck in a familiar boundary. We will experience the rips and tears, and out of fear learn to stay confined within the boundaries. The enemy uses offense to keep you from serving God's purpose and will continue using this same method in your life if it is a familiar place for you to stay stuck. It will take razor-sharp precision of the mind to see clearly between the twisted wires of lies. Razor-sharp vision beyond all the fence line borders is yours to have and God wants it for you. Do not stay bound in the confinement from all God has set aside for you in the next pasture over.

FINAL WORD: I pray that you step through all the wires that satan has used to trip you up, Amen.

BEHIND YOUR BACK

DAY 76

You will be blessed when you come in and blessed when you go out.

— *DEUTERONOMY 28:6 NIV*

You have read a little about my career throughout our journey together here. A much deeper picture needs to be painted of all God has done for me. Have you ever wondered if God showed you all the plans He had for you ahead of time how you might respond? If God had shown me twenty years ago a portrait of my life as it is today, knowingly, without a shadow of doubt, I would have stood in absolute disagreement with every plan He had for me.

Standing still in one place for more than eight hours a day, missed lunches, and unable to have dinner on the table would have left me shouting "that is insane!" If shown the years it would take to establish a clientele I would have responded to God with, "I do not have that amount of time." Showing me my future finances from making four dollars to four hundred, I would have told

Him "nothing less than four thousand please." A glimpse of family, revealing missed weekend events, school and sporting activities, I would have said "absolutely not." Walking me over to picture my body with aching fingers, feet and shoulders, I would have said "that is definitely not for me." Shown my heart from stories and disappointments told while client's backs were turned from me, would have me responding with "it is truly even more than I can bear." Had God shown me my flesh with the marks from burns and the scars from cuts I would have said "you have got to be kidding God."

If God had shown me the beautiful opportunities that would take place to speak of Him, I would have told Him, "I'm not sure that would be the right place." If He would have shown me the countless times I prayed for His people, I would have said, "did I even know how Lord?" Thank God for not offering you and me a picture neither too far ahead nor too far behind. Make a point to thank God for partnering with you in the exact moments of His timing. There is a blessing for you as you come in and as you go out beloved.

FINAL WORD: I pray clarity of being in the will of God means you are in the word of God, Amen.

LIES

DAY 77

"You won't die!" the serpent replied to the woman.

— *GENESIS 3:4 NLT*

Believing the lies can lead us to walking out the lies. When I first began reading the word of God, I remember how the story of Eve in the book of Genesis made me feel. I had at the time thought "how was she so incredibly deceived?" Answer: easily, it is a battle of our minds.

Recently my boys and a close friend they had over wanted to take a little day trip to a trampoline park. Arriving with three high-spirited little boys, they high tailed it straight to the dodge ball pit. I thought to myself, what in the world is fun about being caged in a twelve-square-foot area getting pinged head to toe with balls? Within minutes the boys exited the pit returning to me with cries of slight anger. They asked me to come watch them as problems were happening in the pit with other young children. Some young boys were poking fun at my three and had stepped over the center boundary line taking much closer shots. Kindly, in response to my three boy's cries, I asked them to step out to visit for a brief moment with me. Sharing with them a question into why they appeared surprised by the comments and actions of others, all three replied with what they are saying is not even the truth! In response I answered with, "if it is not true, then why are you surprised or angered by their words?" My boys answered me with, "we do not know." I left them with this before they returned to the pit of pings. Staying calm and having zero response is still a response. Heading back to the pit each took the stance to not reply to the comments and in minutes the other boys gathered their things and left.

How we choose to respond reflects in the truth being flung in our direction. A lie will shake your peace but knowing your truth will allow you to walk away with peace. A lie will also lead to sin, but in order to sin, you must first believe the lie!

FINAL WORD: I pray against the lies In Jesus Name, Amen.

FASCINATED

DAY 78

Then Joshua said to the Israelites, "In the future your children will ask, 'What do these stones mean?' Then you can tell them, 'This is where the Israelites crossed the Jordan on dry ground.'"

— *JOSHUA 4:21-22 NLT*

I am a huge fan of birds, are you? My husband certainly is. In our home he is known as the keeper of the seed. My husband is the one who keeps seed in all feeders and nectar flowing in feeders for the hummingbirds.

One summer afternoon sitting on our front porch I was peacefully taking in God's Word. The hummingbird traffic above my head was extremely heavy that day. Studying the hummingbirds had me instantly noticing the incredible wing speeds they have. They also have an aggressive attitude at the feeder, vocally expressing dominance over their personal feeding domains. On several occasions they would fly forward and backward aggressively, side swiping one another. Catching glimpses of their activity in my peripheral vision while still reading, one hummingbird hovered alone near the porch brick of my home.

This happened more than just a time or two before I got up to take a closer look. Once I could see what was taking place I saw that the hummingbird had been helping a friend who ran smack dab into the wall and was hung up on the brick. Stretching my hand forward I quickly pulled the bird off the wall like velcro. Once freed I watched as both took flight.

Sharing this story with my family that evening at dinner reminded me of the miraculous story in Joshua as the Israelites crossed the Jordan. In Joshua 4:21-22 we are told that in the future your children will ask, and you shall tell them Israel crossed the Jordan on dry ground. Sometimes we all have those had-to-see-it-to-believe-it moments. Then there are the moments when the only witness is the one who shares the sovereign goodness of God. God works in our life and the lives of our loved ones. Retelling the stories of God's magnificent work keeps the memories alive. The Word of God is full of those retold stories of the magnificence of God. Tell your story for generations to come. It is always worth hearing about!

FINAL WORD: I pray all your stories reach into generations yet to come, Amen.

YOKED

DAY 79

Don't team up with those who are unbelievers. How can righteousness be a partner with wickedness? How can light live with darkness?

— *2 CORINTHIANS 6:14 NLT*

I f you own a horse, then most likely you have an opinion about them. Most horse owners have a certain breed or sex they prefer over the other, whether it be a mare (female), stud (male) or gelding (male that has been castrated). Personally, I have little preference other than a yoked relationship. I find little enjoyment from a horse with a hot temper, or one that cannot walk, nor do I enjoy a horse on the run. A horse with a compromised attitude is much more my style.

When I ask the horse to walk, I expect obedience. If inclined to release pressure (giving the horse its head) then the compromise would be to not run away with me. We find this to be true among most of our relationships in life. When I partnered with my husband, I was so certain we were evenly yoked, only to discover we were both more like runaway horses. With the miles traveled by the two of us we have learned that in order to cover any ground together we would need to compromise on several grounds.

The first and most important of all would be engaging in an individual relationship with Christ. Second the relationship we shared in Christ would be the center of our marriage. And last, the influence of Christ we would bring into everything we did. In our relationships we have an opinion on most everything but must find compromise. Making decisions to have a relationship with Christ, center of all relationships outside and inside of home, work and all things drawn out of life should never be compromised or lost in the translation of your opinion. Ask for the Lord to direct your path and send forth the yoked relationships.

FINAL WORD: I pray for yoked relationships, Amen.

FISHER OF MEN

DAY 80

Jesus called out to them, "Come, follow me, and I will show you how to fish for people!"

— *MATTHEW 4:19 NLT*

W hen Jesus called for disciples, He called upon men who were equipped in the trade of fishing. Some men were familiar with the technique of casting of nets and some with the mending of nets. The mending of nets was a tedious technique to repair holes, tie knots and remove debris—the least glamorous part of fishing. If someone is not taking the time needed to do these repairs, the catch would be impossible.

The littlest of tasks can be backed up by the success of big rewards. The casting of nets required the use of a much smaller net thrown to the shallower depths, cascading out and drawn back before sinking to bottom. This technique is still used for small bait. Are you familiar with any of these two techniques?

In the past summers we had taken little trips to the shores of the gulf coast. The seashores always heavily populated during our visits with all kinds of sea life but mostly an abundance of blue crabs. Upon entering the waters, the ocean floor was covered with blue crab leaving many on shore quite fascinated. Blue crab danced with the tides of the ocean currents, dodging tiny toes. Dating back to a particular time on the second day of our trip to the beach, we took notice of the ocean shore lined with coolers, fishing poles, small, large and hand-held casting nets for that day's entertainment. Deciding to join the crowds, we purchased a few hand-held nets and there was the rest of our week's entertainment. Among the larger casting nets being let out, the hand-held nets were better equipped for the job of gathering the sea life. Taking the catches in our nets and releasing them in the coolers along the shoreline led to a question of honesty. Where might we be casting our nets and who are we blessing with the overflow? The safe keeping of our nets and the catch of the day is meant to be shared along every shoreline. Cast your nets and release to others all that God filled them full of. Everyone everywhere needs to hear our big fish stories about what God did!

· · ·

FINAL WORD: I pray for the overflow as you cast out your nets, Amen.

ARROWS IN A WARRIOR'S HAND

DAY 81

Children are a gift from the LORD; they are a reward from him.
Children born to a young man are like arrows in a warrior's hands.

— *PSALM 127:3-4 NLT*

Families across the world have established several customs and many ways their individual households carry on in everyday routines. Personally, mine may look slightly different from yours and yours different than the neighbors and so on. In fact, family customs we experience while growing up may be non-existent for another generation. Having learned of something that is a present custom but may not have been before makes me eager to share with you today.

God and the Word of God is welcome in all four walls of our home and is the established foundation that transforms my household into a home. Having grown up straying far from God led to the creation of a new set of customs. Not just in my own life, but that of my family as well. Hearing about what God did for so many others left me feeling a bit slighted. Quality family ties and peace reigned in my mind for my home but settling for just a household triumphed over that thought. What then would have to change?

God has placed a high value upon multiplying in His word and that leads many to becoming parents today. He still entrusts us with such a precious gift from Him. We should influence our children with the experience of the fullness of life serving God in our homes. The Word tells us that children are a gift from the Lord. Children born to a young man are like arrows in a warrior's hands. How joyful is the man whose quiver is full of them! He will not be put to shame when he confronts his accusers at the city gates (Psalm 127:3-5 NLT).

Take a long look at all the opportunities with the children God has placed in your life. Perhaps they are not ones born to you. Possibly they were passing through so that you may have helped shape a household into a home for them one day. Children are a part of God's plan for multiplying what is good. Revaluate some places that left traces of God not centered in the family dynamic. There you may see a place of breakdown where it was a household and not a home. Will you lend a warrior's hand?

FINAL WORD: I pray God reigns over all family dynamics, Amen.

TREASURES

DAY 82

*The Kingdom of Heaven is like a treasure that a man discovered hidden
in a field. In his excitement, he hid it again and sold everything he
owned to get enough money to buy the field.*

— *MATTHEW 13:44 NLT*

I have received great pleasure and rewards through
serving others. Many times over I have had to count
all my blessings through seeing all the great works
of the Lord. When we take initiative to move where we
see a need, we will always be granted the opportunity to
see the hands of God move. For the last several years I
have partnered with God in ministry serving women of
all ages. From event planning to team building participation, spiritually feeding on the Word, leading others to
Him, and enriching others with encouragement has been
the focus of this ministry.

The ministry has hosted craft nights, conferences and
gatherings of all sorts, bringing forth and calling out
many gifts and healings hidden deep within women.

During one of our monthly events, the idea of hosting a creative rock painting event was inspired by what our very own community had already been doing. Individuals in our community had been placing painted rocks all over town for others to pick up and be blessed with when found.

That one event led many to discover a talent lying dormant. Encouraged, many who were in attendance painted several rocks for themselves after hearing what they could do with them, myself included.

In days ahead my family and I had our yearly plan to head out of town on vacation to the beach. During the long twelve-hour car ride, I had packed several of the painted rocks from that event. Anticipating that there would be many stops along our journey ahead, I placed a rock here and there at various locations. This turned the long car ride into an extremely exciting road trip game of hide and seek. At the end of our vacation while leaving our hotel room, my family took notice of a few of our rocks resting on the front ledge on our last walk by the clerk's desk.

We casually acknowledged to one another with half crooked grins and whispers of thank you, Jesus! Is there an obedient yes that has been suspended until tomorrow? God has a place for your yes to rest. Pull the rocks out of your pockets my friend!

FINAL WORD: I pray for all the thank you Jesus moments, Amen.

CASTLES IN THE SAND

DAY 83

*Have you no respect for me? Why don't you tremble in my presence? I,
the LORD, define the ocean's sandy shoreline as an everlasting boundary
that the waters cannot cross. The waves may toss and roar, but they can
never pass the boundaries I set.*

— *JEREMIAH 5:22 NLT*

The one place I most longed to visit was the
beautiful and majestic islands of Hawaii.
Around seven years ago, the place I had only
dreamed of visiting became the bucket-list trip of a lifetime. A few months prior to booking my trip I had a
detailed dream that almost derailed all my plans. One
night I had awoken a little cautious after seeing in my
dream something in my own heart that I now have
language for thanks to the Lord. The dream that I
initially took as a warning dream was in fact God lending
me sight into what He had assigned specifically ahead for
me. Have you experienced those kinds of dreams?

I flew into Honolulu and planned to spend the next ten days in paradise. My mind raced thinking of the things to check off my list and saw glimpses of that dream. Stepping off the plane and out into the fresh air, breathing in paradise, I had that instant feeling that I had arrived. The first day I was surprised by the island's high cost. Over the next several days I was destined to travel from one end of the island to the other.

A few days into island life I had ventured into so many unplanned stops, taking in the quaintness of the endless shoreline. Scouting out several areas along the shoreline I saw abandoned sandcastles that told of earlier day's activities. Being a west coast girl I was familiar with the turning of tides both high and low. Generally high tide occurs in the morning hours and low tide in the evening hours. The detailed work put into these sandcastles was extraordinary. They were works of art only to be taken out by the tides by morning.

I thought back to the dream I had. In the dream, I had seen a very fragile man short in stature. As I was walking along, I was approached by the man in the dream. The man then demonstrated hand gestures without language. The thought I had interpreted initially through the dream lead me astray to fear, when perhaps the Lord was speaking into the roots of my foundation.

Sandcastles typically take great amounts of time and effort. Can you relate to a sandcastle built in your own dream life? Working diligently in completing the castles in our life will result in wasted time and energy. Anything that requires great admiration that takes our focus from the One to be admired is built on a sandy slope. Is it finances, a position at work, a relationship? There are castles we must build with only God, where other sand-castles cannot exist, and the high tides know the boundary line.

FINAL WORD: *I pray we are Anchored in Christ Jesus when the tides come in waves, Amen.*

WARNING

DAY 84

Your word is a lamp to guide my feet and a light for my path.

— *PSALM 119:105 NLT*

Have you neglected all the warning signs? How are you handling things in life at your own speed? Many highways and roadways across the United States are designated with a speed limit sign. You will also see warnings signs for possible deer crossing, potential rockslides, iced-over bridges, and dead-end roads. When these signs were placed, someone demonstrated the need for caution. The potential of such things happening had to have fallen high on the list for a probable risk to occur.

Recall earlier in the reading of this book where I shared a testimony of a time when my husband had been the candidate for a layoff, just after our major home purchase. Several months before this incident took place the company he had been employed by asked him on a few occasions to transfer to a different area. Have you ever used the phrase "hindsight is twenty-twenty?" This statement means things that are obvious now were not so obvious then.

God has many ways of illuminating His signs for your path. Like a big caution sign ahead, He plans out the safe road. Negligence to obey the caution signs leads us into more U-turns than expected. We are all guilty of heading in our own direction and traveling at our own speed. We could prevent the U-turns from happening if we would heed the warning signs. The path we opt out of taking with God will still lead to a path God will use. God establishes a plan and path for all with fewer U-turns. Use caution in the God given road signs that are illuminating your path ahead.

FINAL WORD: I pray over God lit paths ahead, Amen.

SWEET FRAGRANCE

DAY 85

I am truly his rose, the very theme of his song. I'm overshadowed by his love, growing in the valley!

— *SONG OF SONGS 2:1 TPT*

The sweet fragrance of the rose. Women have strong opinions when discussing floral departments and fragrances. The Bible tells of many scents but there is one most adored, "The Rose of Sharon." In the book of Song of Songs, a love story is written into a poetic song. This story we read is said to have been written as a love dance between God and Israel, perhaps Jesus Christ (the man) for His bride (the church), and last suggested to have been about the marriage of husband and wife (dating back to the garden).

Personally, all sound extremely romantic and I will stake claim to interpret it all three ways. The rose of Sharon and the lily of the valley were flowers found on the beautiful plains of Israel. The woman speaking in a poetic way in this book of the Bible expresses that she is simply a wildflower lily in the valley. The man quickly reminds her of all her excellence among the thorns. Solomon (who possibly wrote the book) described such love on display in extraordinary measures. Another point made is that although the woman does not consider herself anything special, she in fact is the most adorned.

Whenever I was a young girl my grandfather had a beautiful manicured rose garden running the full length of his dirt driveway. On so many occasions that is where he was found carefully tending the garden among all the thorns. I can still picture the hands of my grandfather, the scratches and pricks, and the residue of scabs sealed over with dried blood. Intricate drip lines gave the roses just the right amount of hydration and nourishment needed to obtain their individual beauty. Trimming, pruning and insect repelling left each rose bud intact until full maturity. The vibrant color variations on display in the garden were absolutely astonishing. Dedicated love left its trace aroma from the garden into the home of his wife. There is a union God wants to endorse between you and Him. Just like the tailoring of the rose garden, neatly manicured and cared for with love, I just described for you. We, as the Bride of Christ, should produce a sweet fragrance from the encounters. Jesus Christ has allowed us great opportunity to participate in His beautiful love story. What part of His love story will be written about you?

FINAL WORD: I pray for demonstrations of love, Amen.

RESEMBLANCE

DAY 86

For where two or three gather together as my followers, I am there among them.

— MATTHEW 18:20 NLT

Forever the proudest moment to date in my life is holding the title of mother. I have two amazing, Christ-following young gentlemen. I have shared my personal story and the lack of experiencing Christ while growing up. My husband and I have been obedient in making Christ known to our children. When we are on time and in attendance for Sunday and Wednesday services it should be credited to our children. Our children encourage us to get up, dress up and show up over and over again.

Work weeks are long for most adults and sometimes finding the energy to attend one more thing (that thing being church) is hard for us all. Our children always know just how to draw from the gift of patience when dad and mom have overslept or just flat out missed a service. My children may not have a barometer for any other days of the week but Sunday mornings and Wednesday evening they do. On more than one occasion our children have been a resemblance of Christ-like strength and obedience through their childlike faith and demonstrated behaviors in our home.

Having heard more often than not the well abused statement "it is just church," in fairness it is just church, but a much larger meaning comes to mind when hearing the phrase. Completely true "it is just church," but what is within the walls of church? It is where you have two or more gathered in His name and there He says I am (paraphrased Matthew 18:20). When gathered with the church we receive the power that lends a hand to strength, which leads us to encouragement. When we grow weary and are in need of refueling, the power is found in Him and in the likeness of numbers through His people.

What if I and the entire world reacted to the word play by staying home because "it is just church?" Where would the two or more gather to experience the power, the presence, and goodness of God? We would just be outsourcing our needs to a world that is completely depleted.

We need each other's love, strength, prayers, testimonies and encouragement. For if not the church, what then would help others identify our likeness, struggles and victories? We need an encounter through the words of our testimonies to overcome (paraphrased Revelation 12:11). Assemble my friends together where the presence, the power and victories are heard of and won, just because there is a body of believers called the church!

. . .

FINAL WORD: I cover your church home in prayer, Amen.

DREAM IT

DAY 87

The LORD had said to Abram, "Leave your native country, your relatives, and your father's family, and go to the land that I will show you."

— *GENESIS 12:1 NLT*

In 2004, plunging head-first into faith after honeymooning in Texas, my husband and I decided to move there. Uncertain of the path ahead we had only briefly discussed a time or two how it would be exciting to move to Texas one day. Our travels, just weeks before moving to Texas, while still on our honeymoon, we stopped and explored several small communities. At several of these stops, if the community showed any glimmer of interest to us, we would drop off resumes at the local city buildings.

Back home in Southern California, my husband just out of the military had a very steady job. He was employed by the public works department of the city we lived in. During our honeymoon we made a point to visit Fort

Worth, Texas where we met up with a friend who served with my husband. We spent just a few nights exploring the area and from there we headed off to DFW airport to return home.

Once back home, we made our departure from the plane and checked our phone messages. Much to our surprise we had received a job interview back in Texas. Fumbling our words at the end of the airline ticket counter, we used our leftover vacation dollars to get a red-eye flight back to Fort Worth to interview that following morning. After the interview my husband was hired on the spot and they asked him to start in just two weeks.

When my husband returned home, he went straight to work completing his last two weeks. At the end of two weeks we packed most of our belongings and headed for north central Texas. We stayed with our friends once we arrived, and within four months we both had landed ourselves steady jobs. We were well on our way to purchasing a new home. Something supernatural (beyond explanation) is to be credited for our situation. When we thought about moving, we never dreamed that in two weeks, let alone four months, we would be in a new state and own our home. God challenges us to dream bigger than we could ever imagine is possible. God takes great pleasure in hearing all requests and conversations. God loves showing us that prayers and dreams do come true.

FINAL WORD: *I pray that you have an extra measure of faith to dream bigger than you have ever felt led in believing, Amen.*

EIGHTY-EIGHT

DAY 88

And no one puts new wine into old wineskins. For the old skins would burst from the pressure, spilling the wine and ruining the skins. New wine is stored in new wineskins so that both are preserved.

— *MATTHEW 9:17 NLT*

Throughout the year after weaning the calves born on our home place, we load them up and send them to the sale and the cycle repeats itself. A process happens before they are hauled off. Vaccinating, castrating, branding and ear tagging must be performed on each. This last year having an open schedule gave me time to take part in the day's big events. Ear tags are pre-printed numbered tags placed for identification purposes. That season, the 2018 herd, was a little different than years prior because one calf would walk in the identity of calf number eighty-eight.

At the beginning of that year, the Lord spoke the number eighty-eight into my spirit, following up by repetitively showing me the number in several places, from my everyday purchases to seat numbers while attending events. Communication with God on this subject led me to a vision from Him through the old Disney film *Robin Hood* with the fox, the bear and the rabbits. The fox (Robin Hood) walked into the town's homes disguised as the bear on stilts and collected taxes from the poor (the rabbits). While shaking a cup just as the bear (who was the real tax collector) had been doing, the poor would give all they had. Robin Hood, posing in disguise as the bear, collected all the taxes from the poor only to return it to his people. Does the Scripture "he shall restore sevenfold" speak to you? What had been stolen from them would be given back and then some!

Listening to the Lord's instructions for me about the number eighty-eight, I was directed to put eighty-eight cents down several places throughout the year. Honestly, I had several more questions that were not being answered about the eighty-eight cents but decided the path of obedience was well worth the effort in the end. Have you ever doubted something you knew the Lord told you to do and later seen someone else doing it? The Lord is looking for the ones who will recklessly step out in faith.

Walking into church I would dig in my pocket each week to find eighty-eight cents for the offering, fearful of the sound the coins would make. I left restaurants with eighty-eight cents on the table for a tip, fearful of the looks I might receive. I handed those in need only eighty-eight cents but feared the judgement. Throughout the entire year 2018, I continued in obedience to the Lord, laying eighty-eight cents down.

By the end of the year, the eight-eight cents changed me like an old emptied out change jar having a new appearance. At the end of 2018 clarity came seeing the eights in a new light. Specifically, God has several ways to communicate, and numbers are just one of His several ways. In searching for the answer to my three eights (the year 2018 and 88 cents) I found out this number 888 represents the numerical value of Jesus Christ our Redeemer. Do you fear that God will take from you without returning to you something better? Take the opportunity to empty out and see if He changes your view. We do not put new wine into old wineskins for the old would burst from the pressure (Matthew 9:17 NLT).

Final Word: I pray for new wine skins, Amen.

CONCEALED

DAY 89

For all that is secret will eventually be brought into the open, and everything that is concealed will be brought to light and made known to all.

— *LUKE 8:17 NLT*

One of my favorite childhood games was hide and seek. Like me, I really hope you hated taking the role of the seeker. Who enjoys the frustration in the long drawn-out hunt? It is much more exhilarating to be the one heading off to hide. Many of my relationships with others and all my attempts with God were like a good old-fashioned game of hide and seek. Heading off to hide in my own flesh of sin, I waited to see if I would be found.

Much of my enjoyment was found through my personal lifestyle choices and staying hidden I was comfortable. For the longest time I was completely convinced that I had hidden myself well. I was twelve years old the first time I recall entering into the hiding place of sin with any conscious thought that what I was doing might be wrong. Smokers were all around me and smoking looked like something suitable for all ages to do. Even then, knowing that a strong lack of peace was present in my actions, I chose to ignore the route. Little did I know as a twelve-year old that that would only be the gateway to deception in the game of hide and seek.

These actions continued from there well into a few years out of high school. I continued playing the game of hide and seek sin. Now older and more familiar with sin and really good at the hiding part of the game I had learned that even our best hiding places are always found.

Sooner rather than later, thanks to consequences, we run out of good hiding places. Once we are found we realize there is a seeker (God) who is much better at the game than you or I could ever be. A sense of relief can be found coming out of hiding. God seeks to bring us into the light. Today if you are exhausted from the game of hiding, come out, come out, wherever you are, allowing God to reveal Himself to you.

FINAL WORD: *I pray that the game comes to an end and you come out of all areas of hiding, Amen.*

A CALL TO FAST

DAY 90

Then she lived as a widow to the age of eighty-four. She never left the Temple but stayed there day and night, worshipping God with fasting and prayer.

— *LUKE 2:37 NLT*

At least once a year I feel tugged at my spirit to either complete a fast alone or corporately with others participating. The very first time I had ever entered the obedience to fast, I chose to withhold from food and water for 24 hours. Explaining the thought behind this idea, hairdressers by trade are known for skipping meals. By withholding liquids, we have our best chance of not getting too far behind at work. This intentional fast was much harder than a day behind the chair and completely not for the same reason.

I had read a lot about fasting and making a purpose of it. In starving the flesh, the return was gaining a more intimate relationship with Christ. In the end you certainly draw ever nearer to Christ. Who would not want that, right? After the initial twenty-four-hour fast, and yes I made it, I started a yearly regimen of fasting.

The years that followed I would go into a three-day fast, a seven-day, a three-week and last working myself toward a forty-day fast (note not all were withholding all food and liquid). The forty-day fast was closer to the Daniel fast plan which allowed fruits, vegetables, nuts and water.

Before the forty-day fast, I had some big decisions coming up that year. I personally needed to seek out the heart of God for the matter and rid myself of all the outside noise so He would instruct me on what to do in tough situations. Physically resisting certain cravings was much easier than the battle playing out in my mind. People start a fast for so many different reasons. One may be for breakthrough or healing or to seek out plans for the new year and a new word corporately for churches. Personal needs never outweigh the need simply to lay down our flesh and just get alone with God, entering relationship with Him. Through personal experiences in fasting, I learned a rapid result requires a rapid move of faith. For my part, God asking me to lay some things down to commune in relationship with Him is not asking too much of me. The flesh will always desire the most palatable flavor in life. The greatest battles won are found in the laying down our flesh.

FINAL WORD: *I pray over your individual choices, Amen.*

KNOW HIM

DAY 91

If you had really known me, you would know who my Father is. From now on, you do know him and have seen him!

— *JOHN 14:7 NLT*

Now and again, if scheduling allows, I enjoy road trips to other churches to learn more from Christian speakers. I have formed many new relationships along the way while participating in conferences and church activities. I personally have grown fond of a few and their gift for teaching. Some relationships have given me a great opportunity to mature deeper in ministry.

One story I am sure of will be told for generations. A dear and Godly friend of mine had a speaking engagement planned for herself and happened to be out of state for the whole weekend. I happened to be available and took great pleasure in going along on the road. On day one, session one, we were told that there would be a break before the evening session started up again. Stepping away from the event and heading to town to do some exploring at the local shops was first on my agenda. Parked on the town square, we enjoyed a light lunch and then began to explore the tiny town's stores. The first storefront on our radar was a German-owned shop where we made a few small purchases. Further down sat a storefront with a door having a small mail slot that was still being used for delivering mail. Once we entered we saw from front to back, top to bottom antiques of all varieties. Circling the outer parts of the store, I found myself drawn to a tiny corner where there were stacks of old Bibles. I asked the gentleman behind the counter for a price. The kind gentleman responded "$5 each please." At this point, my friend and I had found exactly what we were after and headed to the front of the store to check out.

There are two things I enjoy more than others. One, old used Bibles, and two old thrift-store suit coats. At the counter the older man who appeared to be the owner of the shop shared how the Bibles had been there for many years. The man further stated he could not recall the sale of a Bible out of his shop in over eighteen years. Striking up deeper conversation, my friend noticed the man had a service hat on and went on to thank him for his service. The atmosphere was feeling a bit closed off and my friend asked the man if serving in the military had strengthened or weakened his faith. In response the man said "both" and that was all he wanted to share about that. Then the man wondered if he might ask us a question. We graciously obliged with "yes." He then asked what our denomination was. My friend spoke for both of us and shared that we were Christians who belonged to Jesus.

Making a few more gestures of small talk, the atmosphere broke. My friend and I, still standing at the counter, mentioned to the man that he did not ask us what it is that we do not believe in. The man said what is it then? "Religion. We do not believe in religion!" was our response. "We believe in having a personal relationship with God."

There was a long pause from the other side of the counter. The man began sharing something that took us both by surprise. He had been a Catholic most of his life and had always gone to church. In the next breath, he shared that he had always attended church, but was sure he had never been noticed. He then shared his views of Heaven. He thought that when he got to Heaven that there would just not be enough room for him. He said how he saw himself seated outside of the gates of Heaven, ushering family right in, but not welcomed himself. With tears rolling down our cheeks, we noticed the Bible laying wide open, resting behind the counter. My friend and I offered a prayer for this man to come to know Jesus in a new way. The man accepted prayer, and rejoiced in continued conversation, to the point he did not want to see us leave.

Before heading out of his shop, taking one last glance back at the man, we said "we will see you in Heaven sir." Wanting to have the last word, the man asked, what are your names? We both responded with "the crazy Jesus chicks" with an ear-to-ear grin and giggle.

The next morning brought us to a local cafe for more Jesus, coffee and biscuits. Reading and discussing that day's devotional, the Holy Spirit began tugging us once more. We headed back to the store that had the door that had the tiny mail slot. We put a signed daily devotional book through the mail slot with the message "we will see you in Heaven, love the crazy Jesus chicks." Would you be so bold as to do something today that might change someone else's perspective of Heaven?

Final Word: I pray that you are the church for the ones who feel unchurched, Amen.

FOCUS

DAY 92

You have always put a wall of protection around him and his home and his property. You have made him prosper in everything he does. Look how rich he is!

— *JOB 1:10 NLT*

I would like to visit today on the well-being of our children who are raised in the world for such a time as this. This keeps me in prayer for God's mercy. With the increased level of child abductions, depression, suicide, abortions and shootings reaching close in all our communities, we as parents are being put on high alert. My parenting has not reached helicopter status, but I must confess it is not far from it.

My children are extremely fortunate to have a father and mother, first and foremost. They are blessed to have parents who are also still together and most of all blessed to have parents who want them. We have always wanted our children and we have always welcomed our children to join in everywhere and everything we do. Having received favor and given the opportunity to attend a small school, they also have seen more occasions for prayer than most will ever see in school.

At the beginning of each school year, local churches pray over all local schools, classrooms, and staff. Large numbers of parents, local community residents, and church members attend in this joyous prayer gathering. The local schools have also made allowances for parents and even staff to initiate a time of prayer at the flagpole. Students, parents, grandparents, community residents, workers and staff gather weekly before school starts.

The school has also designated a prayer locker for our kids to write out a request to have church members in the area pray over them. All prayer requests are taken to church members to then pray over weekly. In the welcoming of God into a place, hedges of protection begin to form over students, parents and staff, beyond the border of the campus. When an army of dedicated prayer soldiers arise asking for the petitions of the community, an enlisted God shows up on the frontline in response. What are the needs that are in your region? Enlist a community of soldiers to wage war against the enemy and watch God place a hedge line of defense.

FINAL WORD: I pray a hedge of protection within your regions, Amen.

THE CLIFF

DAY 93

For she thought, "If I can just touch his robe, I will be healed."

— *MATTHEW 9:21 NLT*

Our purpose and goal in our spiritual walk is to unravel the many layers of healing our souls need with the helping hand of God. Our daily walk together in this book is coming close to an end with only seven days left. I have shared testimonies and my own encounters that parallel stories in the Word of God. I have witnessed and shared with you my own healings through the power of Jesus Christ just like stories of so many others in the Gospels. My own life has been poured out to you to reflect on in the pages of this book. Still there is something that has kept me up at night that I feel you must know. A question that if we were sitting face to face at my dining room table, I am certain you would ask. At what point did you receive your healing breakthrough?

Beloved, it was when I decided to grab hold of the power of faith. There is a place within every human being that longs for that missing piece of the puzzle. When we tap into it, we discover that it was our Salvation through Christ Jesus. When we come into Salvation there is nothing tangible for you or me to see in the physical, right? We took up our faith and grabbed hold of it. We are told in Scripture to walk by faith, not by sight. One of my favorite Scriptures to hang onto is told by my friend Mark in verse 11:24, "Therefore I tell you, whatever you ask in prayer, believe that you have received it, and it will be yours." Is that not how you came to know King Jesus? Are you visiting that place of familiarity now? That's it. That is the same place you tap into for your healing.

Being on the edge of the cliff, waiting for your healing breakthrough is no place for anyone to be. The same place you once tapped into for taking up your eternal gift of Salvation will be the same place you enter with King Jesus for your healing. That is the place you will walk into by faith, and not by sight, believing you have already received it because it is yours.

Look back to riding a bike or driving a car for the first time on your own. We all start out with a little help from a parent, but then there will come a time we will have to believe we can do it as much as our parent believes we can. God is no different in healing all areas of your life. It is not something that God is withholding from you, He is just waiting for you to walk into faith believing that He will do it. Over and over again we hear response after response of Jesus saying throughout Scripture "Your faith has made you well."

I will end today leaving you to read on your own the Bible story of the woman with the issue of blood from our brother Luke. It was not the hem of Jesus' clothes, it was her faith that released healing upon her. If there are roots of disbelief sewn into many layers of the garments you wear, allow God to help those areas become unraveled.

FINAL WORD: I pray that you are attached to the hem of King Jesus, Amen.

HARVEST

DAY 94

Don't be misled—you cannot mock the justice of God. You will always harvest what you plant.

— *GALATIANS 6:7 NLT*

Harvesting what we plant is weighty terminology if we sit for a moment and ponder it. Having participated in different areas of ministry, what I plant carries a greater responsibility. While in attendance for church over a handful of years ago I heard the Lord call me into ministry to women. At first, I had a good laugh thinking I have no business leading women. I had no sisters growing up and limited numbers of women in my life earlier as friends. In saying yes to God to lead women in ministry, I was left feeling totally unequipped and extremely vulnerable (or so I thought).

The career path I chose did lead me to connect to women on a deeper level, gaining great knowledge of what women were in desperate need of. For years, meetings, gatherings and discussions were happening in front of me daily, bouncing back in the reflection of a mirror. So why then would I fear ministry and what God was calling me to do? Because no matter how many hours I clocked, I felt the enemy casting the heavy burden of doubt on me. Some say that God does not call the equipped but that He equips the called.

Each one of us is equipped with a special gift inside for Kingdom purpose. Walking a daily life lead by the Holy Spirit will incline every one of us to hear the heart of the Father. If we listen carefully we will hear Him assign us our purpose so that our gifts may be manifest. All the intricate in-between parts are not for any one of us to worry about. The greatest idea God had was when He made you, He chose you, and He called you for His eternal plan. The plan of God will only work if we partner in assignments He has chosen in our life. Your chapter is only beginning to be written. Be sure to become a moveable bookmark in every chapter of the book God wrote about you. There is a harvest, and it is on the way.

FINAL WORD: I pray you do not grow weary of doing good, Amen.

THIRST

DAY 95

But those who drink the water I give will never be thirsty again. It becomes a fresh, bubbling spring within them, giving them eternal life.

— *JOHN 4:14 NLT*

Have you heard the saying, "you can lead a horse to water, but you cannot make them drink?" That horse they are talking about is a resident on my land. After long horseback rides it is not uncommon for horse and rider to take a visit over to a watering hole or trough. When my husband and I ride we use just one of two watering troughs on our place. For some odd reason, the same two water troughs on our place for years had caused my husband's horse some level of fear. As we approach the trough each time, she snorts, sidesteps, backs up and panics herself so much she misses getting a drink. With much patience, quite a bit of convincing, and a gentle pat of encouragement my husband has finally taught his horse to calm down and gets her to step up, trusting to take a drink.

Understanding what is good for us is not always in plain sight. Let us consider the story of the Samaritan woman at the well in the book of John 4. Jesus was taking a rest next to a well when this Samaritan woman came up to draw water during the daytime hours. Jesus asked her for a drink, and she was so surprised that this Jew was even talking to her. She responded with "You are a Jew and I a Samaritan woman. Why are you asking me for a drink?" Jesus replies with, "If you only knew the gift God has for you and who you are speaking to, you would ask me, and I would supply the living water." As the story moves on, she tells Jesus that he has no bucket and that he must really think he is greater than the ancestors who dug the well. Jesus goes on to tell her that those who drink the water he gives will thirst no more. The woman drops her guard and then begs Jesus for the water. Jesus acknowledges something personal about the woman. Jesus asks the woman to go get her husband. The Samaritan woman replies with, "I do not have a husband." Jesus already knows this about her. She has had five husbands and Jesus tells her she told the truth. Further in the story, Jesus reveals something to this woman. He was not just any person, He was in fact the Messiah!

Are you unaware of which part you fit into regarding this story? Good, let me clear that up. We are all at some point the woman at the well. We all need the everlasting drink from Jesus. All of us have everyday encounters that lead us to the well that God already mapped into His plan for you when He created you. The one resting at the well is Jesus waiting to supply those with a drink. How long will there be backing up, snorting and sidestepping?

Unfortunately, we (myself included at one point) have been much better at sidestepping and backing away from the one waiting for us at the well to quench our thirst. The bucket of lies you have believed may just be the same bucket you will carry to the well and empty out at the feet of Jesus.

FINAL WORD: I pray that you never thirst again, Amen.

SELF TALK

DAY 96

The tongue can bring death or life; those who love to talk will reap the consequences.

— *PROVERBS 18:21 NLT*

Satan can get hold of our mouths and sure make use of our tongues as weaponry. Lending our mouths over to satan is like waking up every day, clocking in and not getting paid to orchestrate his plans. At least when we are working for God and His Kingdom we will be paid back by joining in Heaven. What kind of reward does hell talk of? Let the evil work be in the hand of the evil one alone my friend. Division is one of the goals of the enemy's tactics. So how about that tongue?

Our words can deploy action and cause effectiveness on others whether good or evil. Imagine for a moment the judicial system in this country. Thank the Lord right now we have only witnessed this on television, right? Court hearings that end up on trial have a supported juror. With the majority vote, one simple word spoken, and a person's life can hang in the balance. Words can have tremendous power in saving a life as well. Now I may just be speaking on behalf of the Texas weather forecasts directly, but the words sent out from our local weatherman give warnings to our communities that can be lifesaving advice. Then look at some words leading to death, like words of division and hatred that can lead to violence.

I hope you can agree that these examples put us physically in specific places. What about the tongue empowering our spiritual and emotional state? Spiritually speaking, we have a choice of what enters and what will likely come out. Speak to me with kindness and I know what kind of friend you hang out with—Jesus. The Bible tells us specifically, warning us that we will take responsibility for every word we have spoken, (Matthew 12:36). Our time well spent in the presence of Jesus will help our emotions play a part in what rolls off the tongue. In the end we hold the power on the tip of the tongue to lead with discouragement or encouragement. In choosing the high road, you reflect the One who is higher than the one who represents all hate. Enlist your mouth to exhale the power of life.

FINAL WORD: I pray for the power of your tongue to bring life to many, Amen.

STRIKE THE GROUND

DAY 97

Do not be afraid or discouraged, for the LORD will personally go ahead of you. He will be with you; he will neither fail you nor abandon you.

— *DEUTERONOMY 31:8 NLT*

Road trips can lead to some of the most intimate and memorable moments sitting with God. When I was in my teens and a new driver on the dangerous streets of California, I traveled many miles with the windows down, lost in thought. Do you ever just get so lost in your thoughts while driving that you miss your turn? Not a whole lot has changed in my forties except now I am encouraged to get lost in the presence of God.

In supporting the Godly women in my life who travel many miles preaching and teaching the Gospel, I enjoy tagging along with them now and again. The commute is always a joyful time as we share our hearts with each other, and we talk about our love for Jesus. Before arriving at our destination, something happens. The entire car breaks out in prayer inviting what the Lord would have us do for Him upon arrival.

Have you ever prayed that God would be ahead of you at your destination? It is called extending your personal invite to partner with God ahead of you. When you offer up yourself as His plus one, the ground then is struck because God goes ahead of you. He changes the atmosphere and prepares a heart or maybe hearts to receive an invitation.

Invites most of the time require permission from the host planning what is up ahead, right? The reason is that this gives them time to prepare. When we send out our prayer to get invited along with God, He goes ahead of us and makes all the preparations.

Perhaps we can use another example, one that is extremely familiar to us. Making dinner reservations for you and your sweetheart requires a set arrival time and a name to hold the spot. Would there not already be a place prepared for you upon your arrival? After all, that is the entire point of calling ahead for reservations. God does not need to wait to be your plus one, it is us that need God to be our plus one everywhere. God is the best with all preparations. Are you inviting the right plus one along with you? Be encouraged to invite yourself into whatever it is God is striking the ground to do!

FINAL PRAYER: I pray you bring God your very best and he will simply do the rest, Amen.

CROSSING

DAY 98

Ask me and I will tell you remarkable secrets you do not know about things to come.

— *JEREMIAH 33:3 NLT*

S mall towns have their way of keeping us grounded. The tranquility of family, friends, fairs and fellowship keep most rather biased to their hometown. The one I grew up in lacked sidewalks and stood out as different than most. Norco, California was called Horse Capital, USA.

Along the streets were sand-paved horse trails with crosswalks equipped on each corner. A funny little side note I should share with you is our crosswalks were not pictured as pedestrian crossings. The picture that appeared when it was time to cross was of a horse and rider. Tricky to say the least you had to maneuver on horseback to get to the crosswalk button, angling precisely not to knock yourself off the horse on the crosswalk overhang.

Sitting here writing about this gives me a giddy grin from ear to ear. I had never put much thought into these signs until now. In honoring the person who thought enough about the protection of another, I extend my gratitude. Each day invites several things we simply take for granted in our day-to-day business. God is still in the design business. God gifted something special in each and every one of us. The birthing of that special thing He placed within and created you for and for His use here on earth, is perhaps yet to be discovered.

When he created you in your mother's womb there was already a plan. When He brought you into this world, did you know that you would be the carrier of something great this earth would need? It is true—there is something God has hidden within you to be discovered that this world is waiting for and in need of. Now, beautiful child of God, be encouraged to discover your purpose.

FINAL WORD: I pray for the hidden things God has placed within to birth, Amen.

BREAK FREE

DAY 99

If a man has a hundred sheep and one of them gets lost, what will he do?
Won't he leave the ninety-nine others in the wilderness and go to search
for the one that is lost until he finds it?

— *LUKE 15:4 NLT*

The last ninety-nine days together I pray that you have been encouraged by my personal Gospel encounters with God. I have taken great pleasure in sharing with you many behind the scenes encounters where God has worked in my own life. With only one day left, we have arrived at the end of our time together. While I sit here finishing out today's devotion, I am confident that you will begin your own book of encounters with God.

Today I am pointing you to a well-known story told in the book of Luke 15 about the lost sheep. While the tax collectors and sinners sat together to hear Jesus speak, the teachers of the law grumbled in the company of His presence. We are told of a man caring for a hundred sheep in the wide-open country. When I hear wide-open country the country girl in me flashes to free-range land on the plains of Texas. If just one incident startles the entire herd, it is not going to be an even foot race. Now back to Luke, if one turned up lost what would one man be able to do? Will the one man abandon the ninety-nine in search of the one who is lost until he is found?

I would like to share a more recent encounter of God in search of His lost sheep. There have been days that we all have chosen willingly to stray from the herd (body of Christ). But God has always found a way to direct each of us right back to the herd (body of believers). Recently while sitting in my weekly Bible study with my girl-friends there was a knock on the door. Initially our thoughts went to UPS but at the door an older gentleman stood, hat in hand and head low along with a younger gentleman. The younger man had brought this man to our study after receiving a visit to his place of work. The older gentleman had lost his wife and wanted to give away a few of her items. He went to the younger gentle-man's office where the secretary had a young daughter who could receive these precious things from him that once belonged to the wife. His secretary, concerned for the old man called for the younger man to step into the office and examine the situation. The younger man felt a sense of urgency and knew that his wife would be in Bible study that day so brought him to us.

Once inside everyone could sense a shift in the atmosphere of hopelessly giving up all over the older man's demeanor. The ladies gathered around the older man and allowed him to express how he was feeling and then prayed over him. A lady in the group who knitted blankets asked this gentleman to please meet at the office again in a week where a blanket and several others would be waiting. The next week came and just like what was said, the older gentleman was met with a hand knitted blanket and prayer from our study group.

That Sunday I had entered church and noticed a Bible and some small books on the table in the foyer. As I picked up the Bible and looked through the pages I noticed this Bible was free but belonged to a couple who sowed many seeds of prayer into my own personal life. Thinking that I had found something so precious, my hands gripped the Bible tight. That night reading my new Bible as I went to bed, I was awakened by the Lord with Him telling me to offer the Bible as a gift to someone. I know that the Lord does not wake me, especially at 3:43 A.M. unless He has something to say. In obedience to what the Lord asked me, I got out of bed and posted a message on social media that said "If you need a free Bible message me!"

A few days passed when word came that there was someone who needed a Bible. It was the older man that had paid a visit to our Bible study and had been prayed over. Delivering the Bible, word came back to our Bible study group that the older gentleman had been spotted at their home church with Bible in hand. Furthermore this Bible study lady had invited the older gentleman over for an Easter lunch. The older gentleman seemed to be in higher spirits and God had him on his radar.

A few weeks after the encounter with the older gentleman, our Bible study group had been told that he could use a few additional things to help him out. Our Bible study group got together and supplied him with baskets of things he needed and invited him into the group to receive them during one of our gatherings. Just this last week our Bible study group met with the older man where he felt the need to share some things with the group.

Giving the gentleman the floor to share we learned that this man was a veteran, he was a crop duster for years, he took care of his beautiful wife that he very much adored and was happily married to for sixty plus years. His wife had gone blind four years prior to passing and it was he who took care of all her needs before she passed. For five months he went on to share how he was unable to see her or talk to her because of the COVID pandemic. Broken, this man longed to be reunited with his wife and sadly he had tried to get to her a few times faster than God intended for him to leave earth. The man shared how grateful he was for all of us caring so deeply about him. In fifty years, he had not been to church and with the gently used Bible in hand he was now enjoying the chance to be alive and go on Sundays to Church. He finished by saying how eternally grateful he was to have met each of us.

Do not ever doubt that God is not on a high-speed pursuit of everyone. He knows our locations. There will be much more rejoicing over the one who repents and returns than the ninety-nine who believe they have it all figured out. God sent His One and only Son Jesus to earth in search of the lost. This is an act of extravagant love God has set aside just for us. For you are the one individual, beloved, that God sought to find.

Final Word: I pray you know that you are found, Amen.

UNDER GOD

DAY 100

But if you refuse to serve the LORD, then choose today whom you will serve. Would you prefer the gods your ancestors served beyond the Euphrates? Or will it be the gods of the Amorites in whose land you now live? But as for me and my family, we will serve the LORD.

— *JOSHUA 24:15 NLT*

Here it is, our final day together. Allow me to finish this book with where and who we will serve. We all have big choices to make but none greater than this: who will you serve? In our home on display for all to see is hanging wall art stating "Our house is just a little house, but God knows where we live." Standing on the Scripture "As for me and my house we will serve the Lord" (Joshua 24:15 NLT) is our choice. The choices that impact every tomorrow will be the choices we make for today.

Our future depends on what we desire and what we choose. Personal decisions will match personal consequences. For instance, who we will serve (God) not what we will serve (world). The path we choose will impact friendships, relationships, marriages, finances, children, careers, platforms or church, to name only a few. Something I do often is send my children a friendly reminder before they start their day asking them what team they are serving on today, Team God or Team satan? Thankfully to this day my children still choose to serve Team God.

God intended for there to be order. We are all here to serve under His authority. The order is: God, Husband, Wife, Children, Family, Career so on. In hope I pray you laid your eyes on the first item in that list and got hold of the top one in the order. God requires all you have. God first and everything else after. Keep in mind that if God is not at the top, everything else will fall out of order. Can you allow yourself the opportunity to take a critical inventory of your own life? Is there anything taking priority over God's established order? Are there things in your life serving in a place of disservice to you? What might it take for you to get these things prioritized accordingly? There is an ease in all our days ahead promised to us when God is at the top. As for me and my house we will serve the Lord (Joshua 24:15).

FINAL WORD: I pray for all things to come under the order of God, Amen.

NOTES

ACKNOWLEDGMENTS

1. *Quote By Voltaire "Appreciation is a wonderful thing. It makes what is excellent in others belong to us as well."*

INTRODUCTION

1. *Quote By Voltaire "Writing is the painting of the voice."*

11. LET THE DEAD THINGS GO

1. *Quote By Unknown Author "The trees can show us the importance of letting the dead things go."*

16. WHAT IF?

1. *Quote By Erin Hanson "What if I fall?" "Oh but my darling, what if you fly?"*

17. BEAUTY IN THE SILENCE

1. *Quote By Unknown Author "Never underestimate the power of silence. Some of the most profound insights come from the quietest places."*

23. YOU ARE STRONGER THAN YOU BELIEVE

1. *Quote By Unknown Author "A bird sitting on a tree is never afraid of the branch breaking because her trust is not in the branch but on its own wings."*

28. GOD STILL MOVES

1. www.dictionary.com

32. TRANSFORMATION

1. www.merriam-webster.com

34. THE BEST IS YET TO COME

1. *Quote By R.C. Sproul "There are no draws with God, no split decisions. When we wrestle with the Almighty, we lose. He is the undefeated champion of the universe."*

43. ASK

1. *Quote By Rabindranath Tagore "The one who plants trees, knowing that he will never sit in the shade, has at least started to understand the meaning of life."*

54. I EXALT THEE

1. www.merriam-webster.com

71. EXCITEMENT

1. *Quote By Unknown Author "Things that excite you are not random they are connected to your purpose follow them."*

ABOUT THE AUTHOR

KYLENE CROSSEN is a new author of devotions built from short testimonies of King Jesus in her own life. She is a wife and has been married for seventeen years. Born and raised in Norco, California, she met her husband in 1999 while he was in the United States Marine Corps and married shortly thereafter. She is a mother of two boys and now lives with her family  in the great State of Texas. She owns her own salon and works full time as a hair stylist. On the side she is inspired to write daily devotions. She is passionate in inspiring others to see the marvelous works of Jesus in their own lives. She prays others will become transformed through her testimonies and delve into a maturing relationship with King Jesus.

Through her own encounters with Jesus, she has a heart to draw others into their own personal encounters with King Jesus. Unapologetic and unashamed she is in love with King Jesus and her gift of faith is evident along her travels. She enjoys leading and mentoring while giving herself over fully for the use of the Lord's work in spreading the Gospel. She speaks of the gratitude owed to the outpouring of the Holy Spirit who has given her the tongue like a pen for the use of a skillful writer, for the anointing to bring to the poor the Good News and to proclaim captives be released, and that the blind come to see, and the oppressed are set free in Jesus!

For more information:
Kylene Crossen
xrossenministries888@gmail.com

facebook.com/kylene.crossen2
instagram.com/crossen_photography

Made in the USA
Columbia, SC
14 September 2021